Piet Oudolf's echinaceas and grasses, Millennium Park, Pensthorpe, United Kingdom.

The sumptuous colors of spring, Royal Horticultural Society Gardens Wisley, Woking, United Kingdom.

Japanese-inspired checkerboard patterns, gravel, and mosses in the shade of bamboo canes designed by Ron Herman, Ellison Residence, San Francisco, U.S.

The Odette Monteiro garden, designed by Roberto Burle Marx Petropolis, Brazil.

The straight-lined cypresses and ponds of the Mas de Les Voltes, a garden designed by Fernando Caruncho, Castel del Ampurdán, Spain.

Grasses and topiaries in the Château de Pange gardens designed by Louis Benech, Pange, France.

SERIES EDITED BY ÉLISABETH COUTURIER

CHANTAL COLLEU-DUMOND

talk about contemporary gardens

Flammarion

CONTENTS

PREFACE

From as far back as I can remember, it was in a garden that my real life began—the real life of memories and sensations. My grandmother's garden in Brittany, to be precise, with its patches of mauve dahlias and its paths among the raspberry canes, its borders of pink carnations and its crab apple trees; my first, definitive plunge into scents, color, insatiability, and sheer bliss. I also recall one stormy day when, in an eerie orange flash of light, the lightning suddenly made me aware of the landscape. Doubtless my belief in a vital force dates back to that time, giving life to living creatures, of course, but also to the trees and wind—a "childish animism" that probably still lies deep down inside me and contributes to the wonderment that these green places never fail to stir in me. Michel Foucault said, "The garden is the smallest parcel of the world and then it is the totality of the world." What other place than the garden—embodying both birth and death, the ephemeral and the eternal, every strategy for survival and hence for hope—can focus so much beauty, strength, and frailty? It is indeed a living art, one that plays with time and with the perpetual rebirth of plant life. The garden is what lives on and bears within it the future, often way beyond ourselves. It is definitely one of the few places where I personally feel in total harmony with the world and with myself.

So, for "the lightning flash to last for me" (to quote the poet René Char), to regain those feelings and stimulate my imagination, I have been pushing open garden gates ever since I was a child. I have traveled endlessly in France, from the clipped box hedges of Villandry to the fountains of Versailles, from the water mirrors of Courances to the cascades of Bagatelle, from the azaleas of the Bois des Moutiers to the hellebores of Vastérival, and from the cypresses of Les Colombières to the mimosas in the Domaine de Rayol gardens. I have traveled up and down Italy, from the Borromean Islands to the Amalfi peninsula, from the gardens of Florence to the gardens of Padua. How can I not mention Bomarzo, the Villa d'Este, the Villa Lante, the Villa Balbianello, and all the wonders of the Italian peninsula? I have come under the spell of the Alhambra in Spain, and the gardens of Madeira. In Britain I have walked with sheer delight on the hills at Stourhead and in the gardens of Chatsworth House. I have succumbed to the enchantment of whiteness at Sissinghurst and Hidcote Manor—and let's not forget the gardens of Wörlitz and the terraces of Sanssouci in Potsdam, Germany. Even further afield are the Peterhof Gardens in Russia, the terraces of Amber Palace in India, the floating gardens of Lake Inla in Burma, the gardens of Suzhou in China, those of Ubud in Indonesia, the creations of Burle Marx in Brazil, and a thousand other paradises I have had the pleasure of experiencing. In short, this is an acceptable addiction and I am gently hooked.

My earliest contemporary shocks came from the gardens by Russell Page, which I visited in the 1990s, from the very distinctive layout of the garden rooms at the Villa Landriana, near Rome, and later from La Mortella in Ischia. I also discovered the refined work of Pietro Porcinai in Tuscany. Then came the International Garden Festival in Chaumont-sur-Loire, France, which was a new event in those days. There I enthusiastically discovered Patrick Blanc's vertical gardens, the "cascade of buckets" by Michel Desvigne and Christine Dalnoky, Hiroshi Teshigahara's bamboo walk, Mark Rudkin's white garden, the soft greenhouse by Édouard François, Shodo Suzuki's archipelago, the mists of Peter Latz, and much more—unusual universes, in which beauty vied with humor and inventiveness.

The sheer creativeness displayed at the festival at Chaumont-sur-Loire—of which, whether by chance or by destiny, I am now in charge—made me realize the infinite diversity of possibilities and trends in the art of garden design today, and sparked my curiosity about other forms of gardens.

All gardens—whether ancient, modern, or contemporary—are of interest to me; I find them pleasing and affecting. Trying to assemble these discoveries, even just for contemporary gardens, is a real challenge, especially given the number of different talents at work in such a variety of locations. Despite the difficulty of the task, it is a challenge I have willingly taken up.

Just as photographers "write with light," the landscape architect or gardener writes and composes with nature. Gardens are like musical scores or books, with multiple keys and interpretations. The keyboard is an extremely broad one, involving sight, smell, touch, and hearing simultaneously. The gardens of today will bring you endless surprises, whether they play at reinventing traditions or create their own radically new universes. My job is to bring this incredibly rich landscape to you and—most of all—make you want to stroll around it.

CHANTAL COLLEU-DUMOND

1

DID YOU SAY CONTEMPORARY GARDENS?

21ST-CENTURY GARDENS
GARDENS WITH A DIFFERENCE

A contemporary garden: it sounds like a contradiction in terms. At first glance, our conventional notion of the garden as a place of order, harmony, and unchanging peacefulness is not compatible with the daring, the inventiveness—the extravagance, even—of some of today's gardens.

Without a few clues as to what is going on, we are bound to be disconcerted by Dean Cardasis's Plastic Garden, Martha Schwartz's plant-free interventions, or Beth Chatto's gravel gardens. But how can we not be instantly taken with the sculptural hills of Charles Jencks's Garden of Cosmic Speculation, the strangeness of James Turrell's Irish Sky Garden, or the melancholy of Ian Hamilton Finlay's ruins? How can we fail to marvel at Piet Oudolf's sumptuous compositions of grasses, be dazzled by the magic of Fernando Caruncho's wheat mixed with boxwood, or fascinated by the botanical knowledge and poetry in the creations of Louis Benech or Pascal Cribier? And how can Gilles Clément's Garden in Motion elicit anything but enthusiasm? Or the green belt reconversion of the industrial sites of the Ruhr anything but admiration? How can we fail to be fascinated by the hanging gardens of Édouard François and Emilio Ambasz?

The gardens and landscapes of today have devised new rules, styles, and fashions. While some rely heavily on playing around with codes and forms, endlessly inventing new ways of thinking and experiencing the garden, they nonetheless continue to enjoy a special relationship with beauty, mystery, and grace.

FACING PAGE
Black stones evoking a river in Exchange Square, designed by Martha Schwartz, Manchester, United Kingdom.

The predominant feature is, in fact, diversity—that is, both awareness of an exceptional heritage and the desire to see just how far they can go with new techniques and new plant varieties. Just think of Michel Corajoud's Water Mirror on the dockside in Bordeaux, or Kathryn Gustafson's fascinating fountains at Terrasson, or Vladimir Sitta's cunningly controlled mists in his gardens in Sydney, for example. Today's landscape architects are also reappraising the plants they use, readily choosing new or less common varieties for their graphic or color qualities, plants like sedge, miscanthus, euphorbia, or coralbells, as well as hydrangeas and ophiopogons. Since they also make bold use of spectacular architectures, as in the vertical plantings of Patrick Blanc, surprising innovations like the fleecy clipping of Jacques Wirtz's topiaries, or Marc Nucera's sculpted trees, there is no chance of their gardens all looking the same.

These gardens of today are radically different. Here the conventional layouts seem to have been forgotten, installations seem to override the plant kingdom. Art, architecture, and design are part of the garden mix. The use of structures, textures, and colors appears to run counter to traditional practices. And yet these gardens are all the rage as never before.

How are we to explain this wave of enthusiasm? How do we account for both a major revival of the art of gardening and this increasing public curiosity toward an area that had remained completely neglected for many years?

Paradoxically, before stirring up such interest, this very ancient art, with so rich a history, encountered some serious setbacks during the twentieth century, particularly in Europe. Quite clearly, the garden has mirrored the major crises of that period.

Both during the wartime years and in the frantic reconstruction periods, gardening taste, spirit, science, and know-how seemed to have totally disappeared. People had lost all interest in gardens. During the 1950s and 1960s, nature and the countryside were by no means a central concern for societies as they picked themselves up after those catastrophic events.

Accordingly, in the early 1970s, the garden was in an alarming situation everywhere and actually seemed to be falling into disuse. Large historical gardens were in jeopardy, and beautiful private gardens went untended. At a time when the population of Europe was rising steeply, along with massive migration from the country to the city, cities saw "green spaces" gradually take over, soulless places with no poetry, designed to fill in the gaps in the rampant urban sprawl.

Nonetheless, while the garden had generally fallen out of favor, it was at this time that the profession of landscape architect came into being, and with it the beginnings of a revival.

Some big names in landscaping and gardening gradually came to the fore in the late 1970s, and set about producing some major works, gardens now viewed as benchmarks, slowly restoring this forgotten art to its former glory.

One only has to think of the large geometrical gardens of René Pechère in Belgium, the masterpieces of Russell Page in England and Italy, the remarkable public and private projects of Roberto Burle Marx in Brazil, and the magnificently colored landscape architecture of Luis Barragán in Mexico. So, fresh

talent plying a new trade would play an increasingly important part in rediscovering the art of the garden.

Moreover, and this is a key trend, environmental awareness gradually came into the picture, with concern over the wanton use of the planet's resources. People began to speak out against the devastated forests, the senseless waste, the excessive endangering of biodiversity. In addition to this new environmental awareness, and faced with an overly urbanized world, there came an increasingly strong demand for nature as a balancing factor.

Unquestionably, the start of the vogue for contemporary gardens dates back to the late 1980s. Over 80 percent of the population was then living in cities or suburban areas. The countryside was gradually being drained of its inhabitants. The urban landscape just grew and grew in size. Air pollution, linked to the rising number of cars, became increasingly present in streets, generating a degree of nostalgia for better living conditions, closer to nature. This twofold effect of losing and missing nature is what led to the garden revival.

The taste for gardens benefited notably from the growth of easy transport amenities, shortening distances by rail, road, or air, and bringing previously distant horizons that much closer, thereby totally changing the way people looked at the landscape and at nature. The garden, as a concentrate of controlled vegetation, was the stuff of dreams and escapism, now available to many city dwellers. But what is the garden? For Michel Foucault: "The garden is the smallest parcel of the world and then it is the totality of the world."

As a microcosm, reflecting the macrocosm of the universe, it is often seen as a paradise. Actually, the Greek word for garden is *paradeisos*, the heir to the Persian *pairi-daeza*. The garden is the "place of concord created by God" so that "man and woman might live together in perfect harmony with creation." Indeed, for the great Brazilian landscape architect Roberto Burle Marx, "the garden's calling is to attempt a representation of this miraculous concord. The garden represents the crucial contact of a being with Nature, the right proposition between the small inner world and the immensity of the outside world, so that the balance is restored and tranquillity attained."

Like opera, the garden can be viewed as a total artwork, like the *Gesamtkunstwerk* of German Romanticism, in the sense that it combines several different arts, with architecture, the visual arts, and botany constantly working hand in hand.

This complex alchemy makes a performance of each garden, mobilizing the intelligence, imagination, and sensibility all at once. It is doubtless one of the very few art forms that allows total "immersion" in the artwork, with constant changes of viewpoint, perspective, and lighting. In the garden, not content with just looking in at it from the outside, you get inside the work. Because it represents the city dweller's back-to-nature wish, because it meets the ecological preoccupations of our day, because it conjures up this living world at once full, complex, and fascinating, in these last thirty years or so the

Jardin Plume, designed by Sylvie and Patrick Quibel, Azouville sur Rys, France.

garden has been reaching out to an ever-wider audience. Doubtless, as stated by the eminent garden specialist Michel Baridon, this is because it is involved in "all the mutations of our world view."

What special vocabulary and grammar do we need to learn in order to understand the infinite wealth of the gardens of today and their subtle or conflicting links with those of yesterday? How can we grasp the thread of transformations, evolutions, and reformulations? How do we apprehend the inventions, new practices, and the exploration of fresh territory without getting sidetracked?

It is possible to understand this infinite diversity. Each of us can have an interpretative perspective to find our bearings and obtain answers. You just need to let yourself be astonished, charmed, and carried along by the magic of these new spaces to live in and dream in, these spots for traveling without going anywhere that gardens have become. The aim of this book is to accompany you on that journey of discovery.

GARDENER OR LANDSCAPE ARCHITECT?

Nowadays there are a host of professions and players involved in garden design. Should we refer to them as gardeners, landscape architects, or botanists? How do we distingish between the various designers of gardens and what are the main differences between them?

First of all, what is a garden?

A garden is a sheltered space, enclosed behind a gate, surrounded by a hedge or a fence—in other words, some sort of boundary. The term is originally derived from the Indo-European root *gher*, meaning "fence," which survives both in the Latin *hortus* and in the late Latin *gardinum*. It is obviously related to the German *Garten*, the French *jardin*, and the Portuguese *jardim*.

The word "landscape," which corresponds to something much larger than a garden, comes from the vocabulary of painting and the word "land." The landscape corresponds to the expanse of countryside that an artist can take in with the eye when observing it from a dominant position. The landscape artist was first and foremost a landscape painter.

But, as Alain Roger correctly states, "Land does not immediately qualify as a landscape. From the one to the other, there is the whole process of art." Indeed, this is where the creator's eye comes in, whether he is painting a picture or designing a landscape. We find the same land/landscape connection in every other Germanic language, for example in German with *Land* and *Landschaft*, and also in Romance languages like French with *pays* and *paysage*.

How have garden and landscape-related professions developed over time?

In this area, over time we have moved on from straightforward gardening technique to a much broader view of the professions relating to gardens and landscape design.

In earlier times, all garden-related trades were basically technical in nature. You just had to master the laws of garden maintenance, know the secrets of earth-moving and planting things, be familiar with the rules of hydraulics, optics, and perspective. All you needed to know was how to dig, sow, plant, graft, prune, espalier, water, drain, manure, and fertilize in the manner that these actions were described in the best gardening treatises.

It was in the eighteenth century that gardening became one of the fine arts, with the gardener discovering connections with artists and with the scale of the landscape. Thus, the great English landscape designer Capability Brown—one of the most influential and prolific landscape gardeners—sketched and drew all of his garden projects, like an artist.

Likewise, in the nineteenth century, garden designers, architects, and colorists composed "botanical scenes" with botany lists now called "botanical palettes," which they used in the same way as an artist would use his colors. It was in the twentieth century, in 1948, that the Briton Sir Geoffrey Jellicoe raised the profession of landscape architect to international status by founding the International Federation of Landscape Architects. For him, as an artist, the landscape architect had to be capable of re-enchanting the inhabited world and of evolving "balanced and self-renewing ecosystems" (*The Landscape of Man*). This position was adopted by a few great contemporary landscape architects, including Gilles Clément,

Knotweed (Persicaria) and blond grasses: a Piet Oudolf composition at the Millennium Garden, Pensthorpe, United Kingdom.

for whom the gardener should be "a naturalist who goes as far as possible with and as little as possible against the energies in place."

While environmental awareness and the need to preserve biodiversity are behind one major trend in contemporary gardens, nonetheless there is still a broad spectrum of viewpoints on the art of gardens today, depending on whether their creators are architects working on the scale of the large landscape, artists with an aesthetic view of the garden, or botanists mostly experimenting with plants.

Indeed, today's gardens come into being through the impetus of a wide variety of personalities: architects and urban planners, landscape artists, botanists, scientists, or even entrepreneurs and engineers.

Although the term "landscape architect" is used to cover several different professions, we may distinguish between creative landscape architects like Fernando Caruncho or Piet Oudolf, whose job it is to invent or repair a garden or landscape; landscape architects in urban planning, who are involved in major public works—people like Michel Desvigne, Michel Corajoud, and Alexandre Chemetoff, and landscape gardeners or artists with specialties in plants, like Louis Benech or Pascal Cribier. Probably one of this community's strong points is that there are no clear-cut boundaries between these different professions.

The diversity and wealth of garden and landscape-related professions, in other words the pluridisciplinarity that sometimes leads designers, set designers, and visual artists to contribute to this field, in fact explains the current creative flurry in this area.

Landscape architects today seem to have a great deal of responsibility for two reasons. The first is due to city dwellers' newfound passion for nature, the countryside, and gardens. The second is linked to the gradual destruction of many acres of countryside, disappearing beneath uncontrolled urban development, which is the cause of increased awareness of the landscape.

So, like the building architect, the landscape architect has a key role to play in our society. Like him, he has a "thaumaturgic"—miracle-working—side to him. For Michel Baridon, anyone who designs a garden "plays the role of the organizer, like a god or a demiurge, he turns chaos into cosmos."

Although the landscape architect is tempted to leave vegetation to its own devices, or at least give that impression, clearly the interplay of art and nature is ever present in the garden. It is an unending paradox: nature provides the inspiration, but at every turn it is recreated. This is in fact how Immanuel Kant defines it; it is a matter of reinventing, reconstituting, "ordering the soil with the same diversity as that of nature, but ordering it differently." Actually nothing in the garden is more heavily controlled than the features supposed to copy nature.

Glass and paper partitions in the Calligrâme Garden, Chaumont-sur-Loire International Garden Festival, 2010.

Water staircase in the Jardins de l'Imaginaire (Gardens of the Imagination), designed by Kathryn Gustafson, Terrasson, France.

NEW APPROACHES
NEW PRACTICES

The contemporary garden is by no means insulated from major developments in our societies. It is in fact a faithful reflection of them. Alongside a more aesthetic view, certain crucial sociological or environmental realities of today clearly affect how we relate to the garden and account for new approaches to this discipline.

Thus global warming or disturbances to the water cycle have a bearing on the way we view the garden. While obviously water still has a major role to play here, the growing awareness of environmental issues has generated new attitudes that are more respectful of our natural resources. **Reasonable use of watering, the avoidance of fertilizers, and a preference for native plant species are now becoming increasingly common practice. This is the new creed of many landscape architects: to look for what is beautiful by all means, but also for what is environmentally desirable.**

The famous Gravel Garden by the great English landscape architect Beth Chatto is a highly successful example of a planting in a harsh environment. Sited on a disused parking lot, this development—dating from 1992—is today a benchmark; it can survive extended periods of drought. On dry soil, never watered and badly damaged by heavy visitor traffic, hardy plants such as ornamental grasses, sedums, lavender, rosemary, and poppies have grown magnificently. This now much-imitated garden was the original drought-resistant garden.

PAGES 22–23
Sparkling silver paper curls in the Réflexions (Reflections) garden, Chaumont-sur-Loire International Garden Festival, 2008.

Alongside this more respectful approach to nature, one of the characteristic trends of today's gardens is closely connected with a kind of solidarity. Collective gardens are coming back into fashion. Shared gardens, worker gardens, "plots of land" formerly "made available to family men" by Abbé Lemire in France, these allotments are now making a comeback. **Economic crisis? Mistrust of food supplies? The wish to grow one's own vegetables? Wanting to share gardens with someone else? Since the 1990s, we have been witnessing a genuine "revival" of family or shared gardens. The good thing about them is the way they create links, foster friendly relations, and help people from different generations, backgrounds, and cultures to come together.**

As for the collective urban gardens that began as "community gardens" in New York City in the early 1970s, originally just wasteland turned into gardens, they too have increased and multiplied. The "Green Guerrillas" planted over six hundred community gardens in New York, and thousands more across North America. They are also to be found in Europe, in the shape of "allotment gardens" in Britain, or *Kleingärten* in Berlin and the Netherlands. In these indivisible community gardens, the decision concerning what to grow is taken and carried out collectively. **There are green commandos in Europe, too, known as guerrilla gardeners, carrying out unauthorized plantings to beautify public spaces.**

White heaps of salt in a blue-and-mauve-colored glass garden, part of a tropical garden designed by Andy Cao:
the Glass Garden, Echo Park, Los Angeles, United States.

NEW PRACTICES
NEW MATERIALS

It is primarily from the creative viewpoint that contemporary gardens have seen such an extraordinary development in recent years, notably with the introduction of many new materials and new ways of using traditional materials.

What are we doing in the garden today that we did not do before? The boundaries between art forms have been removed. Anything and everything is put to a useful purpose, with an incredible show of imagination.

Materials are recycled, merged, and matched, timber, glass, stone, fabric, and even metal. Plastics boldly burst in, as in the famous Plastic Garden (1995) by the American landscape architect **Dean Cardasis**, where the yellow and orange and the luminous transparency of this unlikely material triumph amid the plants.

Colored resins and polyesters feature in the works of the American landscape designer **Topher Delaney** in California; in the last few years she has been building "sanctuary gardens," places of retreat and spirituality. But we also find amazing blue glass and steel walls in every shade of the sky and bay of San Francisco, as in the Karam West Residence, designed in 1999.

Another example is the American decorator, who became a master glass artist, **Dale Chihuly**, who regularly uses argon, glass, and neon for the highly colorful sculptures he dots around his gardens, with an unforgettable decor of bright blue arrows populating the reed beds at LongHouse Reserve.

This is also the case with the gardens of the landscape architect **Andy Cao**, who has kept memories from his childhood in Vietnam of enchanted landscapes, which he often recalls with magnificent recycled glass pebbles or shiny shards of granulated glass. The wonderful Glass Garden he designed for Echo Park in California thus poetically aligns small heaps of salt, seemingly floating on the still waters of a salt marsh, amid the agaves and a fascinatingly glossy carpet of blue glass.

As for the work that he created with Xavier Perrot for the CornerStone Gardens in Sonoma, California, its delicate crystal pendants magically sublimate the vegetation.

Water, earth, glass, wood, slate, mirrors, copper, steel, and a thousand other materials: everything is rethought, everything is combined and mixed together. The garden designers at Chaumont-sur-Loire are, of course, in the vanguard of this inventive, bold, even brazen use of new materials and all kinds of scrap objects. There are no taboos, no limits. Nothing escapes the boundless imagination of today's landscape architects.

FACING PAGE

The Fertile Bulbs, designed by Fabien Gantois, Xavier Bonnaud, and Étienne Panien: an example of the recycling of scrap materials to celebrate the exuberance of biodiversity, Chaumont-sur-Loire International Garden Festival, 2011.

DID YOU SAY CONTEMPORARY GARDENS?

2

THE KEY STYLES
AND THEIR CONTEMPORARY VERSIONS

CHINESE GARDENS
PAST AND PRESENT

It may not be common knovvledge, but the Japanese garden—vvhose sober, stark atmospheres are familiar to us all novvadays—is the descendant of the Chinese garden, vvhich passed on a good many of its codes and values. The art of the Chinese garden represents one of the most remarkable forms of art and civilization from the Celestial Empire. Che Bing Chiu described it thus: "The fruit of a slovv gestation, vvith its roots reaching dovvn into the very foundation of the Chinese soul, it is definitely one of the most accomplished forms of artistic expression that the Middle Kingdom has handed dovvn to us."

The traditional Chinese garden is first and foremost a place for living and enjoyment. It symbolizes paradise and seeks to recreate ideal and idealized nature in a miniature world. This paradise has its place at the top of a mountain or on distant islands surrounded by water, where the "elixir of long life" bringing hope of immortality is to be found. This explains the major role—in the symbolism of Chinese gardens—of stones, representing high ground, and water, mirroring the sky and opening out to infinity. If it is an extension of the home, unlike the world of architecture it is characterized by curved lines, asymmetry, and irregularity. In the garden, the Chinese scholar likes to be surprised and to get away from the unbending strictness of rules and rituals.

The Chinese garden complies with two core principles:

—It must **offer an ideal representation of nature**. Its role is to sublimate nature by adapting to rather than imposing on the surroundings. It is meant to seek harmony by playing with the constantly changing vegetation.

—The Chinese garden also has to **make use of "borrowed landscapes,"** such as mountains, represented by rocks, or the sea and lakes, suggested by water. The presence of scenes evoking another place is a major feature of the garden, which then becomes a place combining two spaces, the here and the elsewhere; the one being seen, the other being suggested.

Feng shui is a key feature of the traditional Chinese garden. This principle, seeking to balance the forces of nature, with man in harmony with his environment, literally means "less is better," thereby placing quality before quantity. It leads to discovering the main elements of the garden environment and locating its negative and positive aspects, for the garden is vvhere this osmosis occurs as man and nature meet. Respect for the environment, a site that blends in, the protection of water sources and courses, the preservation of plants and trees, in a word a setting where the VVay of Man and the VVay of Heaven are in harmony, such is the architect VVang Qi-Heng's definition of feng shui.

Unlike in VVestern gardens, the Chinese garden is not intended to create a "botanical collection." However charming the apricot or almond trees or the ginkgo bilobas adorning the garden may be, the prime purpose of

trees and shrubs is to open up interesting vistas. Plants are used more for the poetry they exude, like chrysanthemums or peonies, or for the symbols they express. Thus vines, peach trees, and bamboo all represent longevity. Lastly, the Chinese garden obeys the laws of yin and yang: in China, beauty and plainness, light and dark are the chief components of harmony. Craggy rock formations represent the yang force, while still water expresses the yin.

The archetype of the traditional Chinese private garden is located near Shanghai, in Suzhou, a charming town reminiscent of

Venice with its numerous canals. This was formerly, in the fifth century CE, the capital of the Wu kingdom. Unlike the large imperial gardens with their fairly regular design, the classic gardens of Suzhou are characterized by their intimacy, delicateness, and inventiveness. Bearing some highly evocative names—the Master of Nets Garden, the Great Wave Pavilion, the Humble Adminstrator's Garden—they are the reflection of an extremely sophisticated civilization. Designed during the first half of the sixteenth century, the last-named, also known as the Policy of the Humble Man Garden, with its meandering streams, arched bridges, poetic pavilions, covered galleries, and moon-shaped gates, is one of the most famous gardens of the set, and became a UNESCO World Heritage Site in 1997.

Nowadays, how is the tradition being revived and by whom? While the twentieth century in China did not encourage a special relationship with the natural and architectural heritage of the country's age-old civilization, for political reasons, as we know, and also after the wanton destruction of ancient sites and neighborhoods due to high-density urbanization, we are witnessing **a dawning awareness of the treasures of the past and a revival of landscape art. There are also, in this field, great talents emerging, seeking to return to the memory of Chinese culture, and contributing with a new approach—at once environmentally friendly, human, and imaginative—to accompany the exponential growth of China's cities and economy.**

In this way certain themes or constants of traditional Chinese gardens are being updated and reinterpreted, with the free eye of landscape architects reinventing the codes as they bridge the years of deliberate oblivion. **Such is the case with Wang Shu, Yu Kongjian, and Wang Xiangrong.**

Born in Hangzhou, southern China in 1963, Wang Shu, a multitalented architect and landscape artist, belongs to a group of young designers advocating a new approach to their profession, based on sustainable construction that is both profoundly humanistic and environmentally friendly. This versatile personality, an architect and writer, teacher and philosopher, describes himself as being "in search of a modern identity for China that does not renege on its own civilization.... I was a writer before becoming an architect and architecture is only one part of my work. For me, humanity is more important than architecture and low-tech is more important than high-tech." This is how, by reusing the materials of traditional homes and gardens, Wang Shu works on memory and reappropriates the past. For building the fine art school campus in Hangzhou, this advocate of the slow-build approach salvaged stones and tiles from the city's old quarters, knocked down during the uncontrolled development that destroyed the heritage. Those same tiles were reused to design the garden that he presented at the 2006 Venice Architecture Biennale: 66,000 tiles to create an "experimental garden," advocating recycling. By using materials from the past, whether salvaged or local craft products, Wang Shu successfuly makes the connection between ancient and modern in a manner at once critical, splendid, and contemporary. He was awarded the Pritzker Architecture Prize in 2012.

Meanwhile, with extraordinary inventiveness, Yu Kongjian revisits the basic concepts of the traditional Chinese garden, such as feng shui, of which he is a leading exponent.

A peasant's son born in Zhejiang province, Yu Kongjian went to Beijing Forestry University in 1980, and naturally enough decided to major in "landscape." For a few years he taught in the Chinese capital, before moving abroad. In 1997, on returning home from the United States, having earned a PhD in design at Harvard, he set about founding the first landscape school, which came into being in 2003. A founder of the Turenscape agency, which has its headquarters in the Chinese capital, he heads the landscape department at Beijing University. He is also editor in chief of a magazine devoted to landscape architecture.

An architect and leading landscape designer who is keenly concerned about the ecological problems facing his country, and well aware of the disappearing forests, the exhaustion of water supplies, and the destruction of farmland, he advocates landscaping projects that are both beautiful and entirely environmentally friendly, in which man can find a suitable place.

Jiangyangfan Eco-Park, designed by Wang Xiangrong, in Hangzhou, China.

His emblematic creation is the extraordinary length of red fiberglass ribbon that he deployed across some urban wasteland in the suburbs of Qinhuangdao, making sure not to raze everything to the ground and spill out tons of concrete, as the alternative projects were recommending. Total immersion in nature, minimal impact on the environment, minimum cost and building time, maximum beauty and poetry—these words sum up this highly delicate and remarkably aesthetically effective project, which was greeted with unanimous acclaim by the local population.

In another of his major works, on the architecture university campus at Shenyang in Liaoning province, reinventing the art of the old pavilions, he was content to design convivial wooden terraces, places for meeting people or for meditating among the paddy fields, inviting students to enjoy an enthralling dialogue with the elements, given that feng shui involves understanding the deep energies contained in places.

Another key figure in the Chinese contemporary garden, **Wang Xiangrong**, born in 1963, professor and vice-dean of the School of Landscape Architecture at Beijing Forestry University, is the head landscape architect at DYJG Studio and editor in chief of a magazine devoted to landscape architecture. He is considered one of the most brilliant landscape architects of his generation. After studying at Tongji University, graduating from Beijing Forestry University in 1986, he earned a doctor's degree from the School of Urban Planning and Landscape Planning at Kassel University in Germany in 1995.

A guest of the Chaumont-sur-Loire International Garden Festival in 2011, Wang Xiangrong designed a work that was radically contemporary in the choice of materials to use (metal, wood, fabrics, etc.), and yet totally complying with the rules of the traditional "misty" Chinese garden with its blue and white ribbons representing the sky and clouds, its red pavilions, the presence of water and the magic of hundreds of little bells tinkling in the breeze.

Between Sky and Earth garden, designed by Wang Xiangrong for the Chaumont-sur-Loire International Garden Festival, 2011.

While they are central to the landscaping work of a new generation of Chinese landscape architects, the stereotypes of the traditional gardens of the Middle Kingdom have also had an influence on some landscape designers in the West. Thus the great Dutch landscape architect Adriaan Geuze had fun creating a masterly reinterpretation, for the Xi'an International Horticulture Exhibition of 2011, of the poetic red bridges to be found everywhere in Chinese calligraphy and garden architecture. Designing an extraordinary Garden of 10,000 Bridges, he takes visitors over undulating red concrete arches straddling a thick jungle of bamboo, and symbolizing life's ups and downs. Meanders, mazes, troubled waters, and stumbling blocks for finding one's bearings are placed with consummate skill along this aesthetic and metaphorical nature trail.

Red ribbon following the riverside path—landscape created by Yu Kongjiang at Tanghe River Park, Qinhuangdao, China.

JAPANESE GARDENS
PAST AND PRESENT

As heirs of the Chinese garden, but having staked their own identity over time, the traditional Japanese gardens of temples, graves, and private mansions are no less important an art form than calligraphy, with very precise aesthetic codes. Called "the art of erecting stones," a sign of the importance of its mineral element, the Japanese garden has fully assimilated the science so dear to the Chinese of "the balancing of the forces of the universe" (feng shui).

No doubt the Japanese aristocrats who created the country's earliest gardens were also hoping to win prosperity and long life by following these "rules" for "living in harmony with the universe." The very first gardens, the Shenden-type (eighth to twelfth century), blending in perfect harmony with the architecture of the day, were composed of islands and ponds. The customary way of exploring them was in fact by sailing round them in small boats on the surrounding lake. **Buddhism, which was imported from China via Korea in the third century and became the state religion in the sixth century, played a key role in society and in how Japanese gardens developed. Bearing a feeling of melancholy and wistfulness in troubled historical times, this was translated in aesthetic terms through important concepts and feelings such as the "impermanence of things," "the beauty of the fleetingness of life," and the**

melancholy it gives rise to. The gardens linked to that religion are unquestionably the ones that most mark "passing time," the course of the seasons, through the planting of trees and shrubs connected with these emotions, like the "four seasons garden" Shikitei, in which maples and cherry trees, with their riveting colors in the landscape, herald the changing weather and seasons. The basic principles behind these gardens, inherited from the Chinese gardens, are the reproduction of nature in miniature, symbolism, and the representation of landscapes.

The nobility were not the only ones to take an interest in the art of gardens. At the time of the Fujiwaras (eighth to twelfth centuries), two esoteric Buddhist sects—the Tendai and Shingon schools—saw their monks, who were also learned men, take an interest in creating gardens inside their temple and design very tiny spaces compared to those of the nobility, while ignoring the "enjoyment" aspect and the reference to poetry. Under the influence of the Zen aesthetic, this was, for the monks, a way of implementing the idea expressed by William Blake, "to see a world in a grain of sand." These new **karesansui** or **dry landscape gardens** (often called Zen gardens), built solely for looking at from the buildings, are very graphic arrangements of rocks, gravel, and moss, with the odd tree or shrub. The art of gardens is here closely related to painting: these utterly austere dry landscape gardens are called upon to interpret and idealize nature, and make reference to classic themes with the use of mineral elements, such as boulders representing mountains, and raked white sand on the ground evoking waves on the water. But in some cases, the subject matter is completely different, and such gardens are used to illustrate some sacred words, idea, or special moment in life. They are teaching aids

Moss Garden (Koke-dera), founded in 731 by the priest Gyoki and rebuilt in 1339 by the priest Soseki, in Kyoto, Japan.

for novices. The vast expanses of raked gravel, as at Ry ōan-ji, serve as an exercise in concentration for the monks, the first step towards hopefully controlling one's mind and attaining serenity.

So the *karesansui* is a landmark moment in the development of Japanese gardens and is one of the profoundly "visible" traces of the influence of Zen Buddhism on society. Rather than recreate an "accurate copy" of nature, the monks seek to convey its essence, even through the garden. Hence we pass from mimicry to symbolism verging on abstraction.

During the development of these dry landscape gardens, the gardens of the nobility and wealthy lords continued to advance, with some highly poetic atmospheres and notably delicate paths marking the birth of a new archetype, called the "stroll garden."

In the sixteeth century the importance that tea was to have in Japanese society led to new forms of architecture and gardens linked to the special "tea ceremony" ritual. Gardens became more natural, more sober, more spare. They had to evoke a mountain path leading to a hermitage, and so became the setting for the tea ceremony. The garden was no longer a place for contemplation, becoming a path of initiation instead. The tea gardens are doubtless the most Japanese of the Japanese gardens.

In all cases, miniaturization leads to "reduced complexity," simplicity being a key characteristic of Japanese gardens. The plants, placed asymmetrically so as to allow the visitor's gaze to wander freely, serve either to conceal or to highlight certain areas of the garden. A few small, fine trees, carefully chosen for their original shapes, gnarled black pine or arborvitae trimmed into cloud shapes, are the only vegetation allowed, apart from moss. The Japanese garden concept is such that it has to be viewed with "higher" vision, without thereby commanding a full view of the entire garden. For aesthetic reasons these gardens are never entirely visible; concealing certain elements depending on the point of view makes the garden more interesting, and makes it look bigger than it really is. This may also be seen as a metaphor for human existence, where it is never possible to know the whole truth.

How are the codes of the traditional Japanese garden reinterpreted today? How is it adapted to the contemporary world? Several key figures have contrived to combine Japan's traditional identity with a contemporary vision of the landscape and of gardens, one of them being a personality who cannot be overlooked. **Indeed Mirei Shigemori brilliantly embodies the dual principles of the contemporary Japanese garden, at the crossroads between tradition and openness to Western influences.**

Born in Yoshikawa in 1896, Mirei Shigemori, who died in 1975, was a writer, a specialist in traditional Japanese gardens, and a landscape architect; he is a key figure in the world of gardens in Japan. Steeped in his country's traditional culture, and well versed in the tea ceremony and ikebana, the Japanese art of flower arranging. Between 1930 and 1932, after studying art in Tokyo, he published some very scholarly books on ikebana and traditional Japanese gardens. His first major commission came in 1934, for the garden at the Kasuga-Taisha sanctuary at Nara. In 1938–39, he undertook a detailed catalog of over 250 gardens in Japan. His first major work was the recreation of the Tofuku-ji temple garden in 1939. Working free of charge in exchange for total creative freedom, he thus laid the foundations for his project to renew the art of the Japanese garden, its emblem being the famous checkered pattern of stones and mosses in the building's western garden. From 1940 to 1949, he spent most of his time writing, publishing thirty-three books. In constructing his most avant-garde gardens, Shigemori embodied a major artistic quest of his day. He marked a new direction in Japanese creativity, based on the desire to overcome the fundamental tension opposing the dynamic influences of Western culture and the permanence of Asian traditions.

Considering this bipolarity to be extremely fertile, and that the dichotomy between "Japanese tradition" and "Western modernity" needs to be transcended, in his gardens Shigemori is sensitive both to the primordial power attributed to nature by the Shintoist tradition and to the methods and resources of his own time. Hence he advocates a hybrid approach, whereby the past inspires without hampering invention, and without preventing formal innovations, and champions the use of unusual colors or novel materials, such as

Karesansui or dry landscape garden, designed by the landscape architect Shunmyo Masuno in Marzahn Park, Berlin, Germany.

concrete for instance. To him we owe 240 gardens of fascinating, timeless beauty, the *karesansui* or dry landscape garden offering a remarkable synthesis of tradition and the contemporary vision. Among his most influential completed projects are Tofuku-ji in Kyoto (1939), Kishiwada-jo in Kishiwada, the Osaka Prefecture Garden (1953), Zuiho-in in Kyoto (1961), Sumiyoshi Jinja in Sasayama, Hyogo prefecture (1966), and Matsuo Taisha in Kyoto (1975).

Another key figure in this Japan–West connection is **Isamu Noguchi**, born 1904, died 1988, the son of the Japanese poet Yoneijiro Noguchi and the American writer Leonie Gilmour. His dual culture, and his medical and sculpture studies turned him into a very rounded personality, his life a succession of trips from East to West and back again. Isamu Noguchi is the author of an extremely multi-disciplinary oeuvre open to the other arts. He worked as much for the world of theater as for the contemporary dance scene, notably collaborating with the choreographer Martha Graham. Working in New York, Los Angeles, Tokyo, Sapporo, and Paris, designing stage sets as well as sculptures, objects, and furniture, most notably his well-known paper lamps, he also designed a number of gardens (the Billy Rose Sculpture Garden at the Jerusalem Museum, the Kodomo no Kuni children's garden in Tokyo), including the UNESCO Garden in Paris. **Rather than slavishly copy tradition, he introduces a new form, achieving an unusual alliance of man, architecture, and space. Thus his Paris garden is visible in its entirety to the visitor, which is never the case with a traditional garden. Likewise, this garden clearly runs along three lines, which are invisible in the gardens of Kyoto. Running counter to the customary codes, Noguchi also introduces tarmac into his garden as a visual gesture.**

Through his art, man takes control over nature in the garden. This is a crucial feature of contemporary Japanese gardens: human creation takes precedence over nature and tradition.

Shunmyo Masuno is another larger-than-life character in Japanese landscaping: a landscape architect, an academic (Tama Art University), and a practicing Zen Buddhist monk, in charge of the Kencho-ji monastery. He is extremely prolific, having designed many gardens both in Japan and in other countries. His gardens are very contemporary in style, linked to tradition and yet perfectly grounded in today's world through his use of the techniques and materials of his day, and they bear the stamp of exceptional spirituality.

For Shunmyo Masuno, the garden is not just any place where flowers are planted. It is a place where the spirit lives. Gardens are "expressions of the mind" of their designer. The garden, like poetry, allows feelings to be expressed which cannot be directly understood or conveyed. The garden is "self-expression."

For Shunmyo Masuno, a successful garden is another self, a mirror of the mind. So for him, the garden is an extraordinary place to engage in spiritual training. The numerous private gardens, hotels, and public places he designed are amazingly daring and extremely beautifully drawn, as well as remarkably powerful.

FACING PAGE

Fountain and Kojimachi Kaikan Zen garden designed by the priest and landscape architect Shunmyo Masuno, Tokyo, Japan.

ITALIAN GARDENS
PAST AND PRESENT

The Italian Renaissance marked the beginning of a new art of the garden. While such features of the medieval garden as lawns, tree-covered walks, and fountains did not disappear, sixteenth-century Italian gardens underwent an extraordinary transformation. Designed around huge villas by teams of versatile artists inspired by the humanist revival, they now formed part of vast estates. They were equipped with wide terraces opening onto the horizon, laid out on hillsides or river embankments, as on the Arno in Florence. Ancient sculptures were used to decorate their broad vistas.

A major novelty in these Italian Renaissance gardens, for the first time the rule of number, the mathematical division of space, came into its own. Geometry imposed its law—even upon the vegetation. Another key element was the soothing presence of water, in the shape of ponds, waterfalls, and fountains. The vistas out to the horizon from such gardens were composed like Italian Renaissance paintings. Like them, they reflected that ideal of humanist thought: openness.

With its five glorious terraces, the Villa d'Este in Tivoli is one of the best-known gardens from this period. Building work was started in 1555–60 by the architect Pirro Ligorio for Cardinal Hippolyte d'Este. Its multiple terraces, giving the overall impression of a single frontage divided into five superimposed "orders," with countless water fountains, colonnades, steps, and mossy grottoes, lined with oak trees, cypresses, boxwood, and wisteria, are of unrivalled sumptuousness and poetry. We must also imagine water-powered automata in these gardens, adding a playful dimension to the stunning concert

FACING PAGE

Villa Gamberaia, where the magic of yews and lemon trees is mirrored in the ponds of the terrace overlooking the Arno Valley, Settignano, near Florence, Italy.

of springs and cascades. Villa d'Este is one of the earliest *giardini delle meraviglie* (gardens of wonders).

Another example of these classical Italian gardens is the Vatican's Belvedere Courtyard, designed by Bramante, with its geometric lines, the presence of ancient works, and its monumental flights of stairs. Outstanding among the many gardens of that time are the Villa Pratolino garden near Florence, designed in 1568, with its colossal statues of giants, the Boboli Gardens (the gardens of the Pitti Palace), with their numerous fountains, grottoes, and allegorical statues, and the sublime Villa Gamberaia gardens in Settignano. Near Sienna, the Villa di Fagnano gardens, and at Castelnuovo Berardenga the Villa Chigi gardens, further illustrate this accomplished art of the Italian garden—green, peaceful, symmetrical, and regular in shape.

Palaces and stately homes are surrounded by countless extraordinary gardens, which have lived on for centuries without losing any of their beauty. The heritage in Italy is so overpowering that art

sometimes seems to be tradition-bound. What twentieth- and twenty-first century gardens have been created in Italy? Often, twentieth-century gardens have evolved under the impetus of foreign-based talents, like Russell Page at the Villa Landriana gardens near Rome, or the La Mortella Gardens at Ischia; or Cecil Ross Pinsent at the villas I Tatti and La Foce in Tuscany. One notable exception, though, is Pietro Porcinai (1910–1990), the son of the manager of the Villa Gamberaia gardens. A well-known artist and designer, he was one of the finest landscape architects of his day.

Very early on, he met the Englishmen Russell Page and Geoffrey Jellicoe and the Belgian René Pechère. Noticing how Italian landscape art education was too strongly weighted in favor of historical tradition, he very soon came out against the common wisdom, pleading for interdisciplinary cooperation between building architects, urban planners, artists, and landscape architects. He worked a great deal abroad, notably alongside Renzo Piano on the Centre

PAGES 42–43
An open-air theater overlooking the Tuscan countryside, in the Villa l'Apparita garden, designed by Pietro Porcinai near Siena, Italy.

Pompidou in Paris. In Collodi, he had a hand in making the Pinocchio Park, with its mazes covered with climbing ivy, and thickets of bamboo and pittosporum. He also worked with Oscar Niemeyer on building the corporate headquarters of the Mondadori publishing house in Segrate. He recommended a careful attitude to the environment, notably attaching great importance to the issue of conserving water; he was a trailblazer in this respect. Porcinai's vision drew strength from three core principles: the relationship with the surrounding landscape, a clear preference for the use of native plant species, and the harmonious integration of pools and ponds within the landscape. Influenced by the work of Burle Marx, he adopted squares and rectangles; he also designed oblong swimming pools and tangles of footpaths. Highly sensitive to the heritage of the great Renaissance gardens, he is to be seen as an "ancient modern," subtly blending boxwood and concrete.

FRENCH GARDENS
PAST AND PRESENT

Inspired by the Italian model, the *jardin à la française*, or French garden—also known as a formal garden or regular garden—is based on geometric lines and promotes the art of order and symmetry. It lays the emphasis on grand vistas defined by vast terraces and broad, straight paths. It makes lavish use of plants clipped into regular shapes, impossible to be found in nature.

It was Nicolas Fouquet, the superintendent of finances under Louis XIV, who had the first French garden planted at his château in Vaux-le-Vicomte (1656–61), with André Le Nôtre, who was to become the greatest "gardener" of his day. Spacious terraces, a vista from the château extended by a canal, and water everywhere make this garden the symbol of the triumph of mind over nature.

The grounds at Vaux-le-Vicomte were in a sense a dry run for Le Nôtre, before he embarked on the Versailles project, considered the most accomplished example of the formal garden. With Louis XIV's coronation and his taste for grandeur, the garden was to play a political role and underscore the king's power. Order had to triumph over the disorder of nature.

At Versailles, everything is controlled, with nothing left to chance. From the château terrace, visitors had to have a complete picture of the garden's overall architecture. Everything was ordered on the basis of the main viewpoint from the king's chambers. A central path marks the perspective and forms the backbone of the design. On either side of this axis, pathways, *parterres de broderie* (embroidery-like ornamental gardens), ponds, bosks, and avenues of trees are organized. The arrangement is divided into garden rooms, each serving a different purpose, along a pre-established

walk. Statues and topiaries are elegantly dotted around these *chambres de verdure*, with long paths edged with hornbeam hedges or fences. With some extraordinary scenic arrangements, mirror-like ponds and cascades like crystals chandeliers vie in magnificence with each other. Beyond the amphitheaters, mazes, lawns, trellises, porticoes, and clumps of full-grown trees, nature gradually comes back into its own in the shape of woods and meadows, as one moves farther away from the château. Surrounded by the top specialists of his day in optics, hydraulics, and botany, Le Nôtre, in a harmonious blend of strictness and sensitivity, oversaw this giant works program with a vision and systematic mind that were out of the ordinary.

Many gardens designed with such art appeared in France during Louis XIV's reign. The Château de Chantilly, the Parc de Sceaux, the Parc de Saint-Cloud, and the Tuileries Gardens in Paris number among the finest gardens of the period.

Many royal courts of Europe took inspiration from the French model, which has been maintained over the centuries, with many historic gardens having been beautifully kept right down to the present day.

But who were the heirs to this very unusual style that has occasionally fallen out of vogue due to passing time and outside influences?

FACING PAGE
French perspectives, with straight paths and parterres, in the grounds of the Château de Vaux-le-Vicomte, France.

The great French landscape architect Henri Duchêne (1841–1902) in the late nineteenth century built up a prestigious clientele among the landed gentry. His landscape work is characterized by its tastefulness, which he passed on to his son Achille Duchêne (1866–1947), and for the return to the tradition of seventeenth-century French gardens. He worked in this manner on projects at various stately homes, including the Château de Bauderies, Château de Vaux-le-Pénil, Château de Breteuil, Château de Bouges, and Château de Chaumont-sur-Loire.

Also, certain formal gardens, for example at Villandry and Eyrignac, have been either reconstructed or reinvented by their owners, with a degree of creative distancing from the established codes.

Thus at Eyrignac, in the Périgord region, on retracing the original outline, the owners followed their own inspiration and redesigned a verdant garden in every shade of green. In this spot, plant sculptures, boxwood *broderie*, garden rooms, and parterres revert to the influence and balance of the classical garden. At Villandry, too, the fantasy of the garden's "refounder," Joachim Carvalho, and his successors, has contrived to play around imaginatively with the garden's original structure. Another example is the decorator

PAGES 46–47
Deciduous and evergreen hedges in alternation: a reinterpretation of the classical rules at the Château d'Eyrignac, France.

Jacques Garcia's very loose reconstruction of the French-style grounds at Champ-de-Bataille.

Among the great twentieth-century French landscape architects, **Allain Provost**, born in 1938, and the designer of many contemporary parks and gardens in France and elsewhere, is a self-styled exponent of "unashamed classicism," working in the tradition of the *jardin à la française*. For this prolific landscape architect, who designed the remarkable Parc André-Citroën in Paris, as well as the Parc de La Courneuve, and the Parc Diderot in the La Défense quarter of Paris, "geometry and compositional axes are basic landscape features.... Geometry is a tool of prime importance with which to bring back into our cities simple outlines that break up their increasingly haphazard urban sedimentation effects.

"A project is a powerful idea introduced by a geometry and tempered by some nicely careless touches and harmonious flights of fancy that make its outline and charm."

Although extremely prolific, contemporary French landscape architects do not especially claim to follow this geometric tradition; conversely, some leading American landscape architects like Dan Kiley (1912–2004) openly admit to being influenced by the *jardin à la française*.

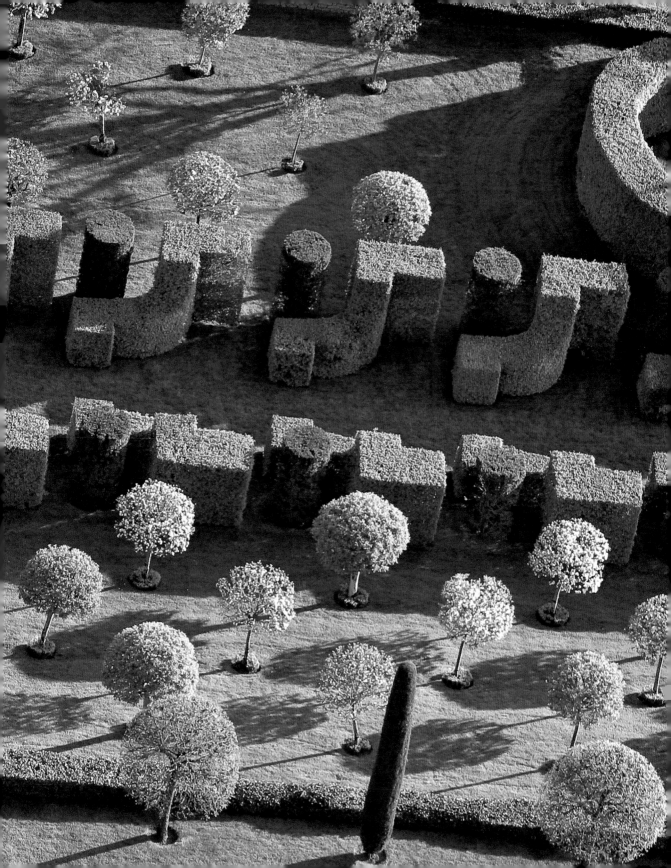

ENGLISH GARDENS
PAST AND PRESENT

If there is one country where the art of the garden is one of life's essentials, it is, of course, England. The "English garden" concept first appeared in the eighteenth century, when the art was in its heyday. During previous centuries, the English were mostly influenced by Italian and French gardens, with their geometric formalism and symmetrical patterns, straight paths, tidy thickets, and parterres. That is, until two major figures, Charles Bridgeman and the painter William Kent, cast these continental conventions to the wind and transformed the English garden.

Charles Bridgeman (1690–1738), who was responsible for restoring the royal gardens, called into question the symmetrical organization of the grounds, and rejected the fashion for clipping trees, until then systematically trimmed into the shape of a cone, ball, or pyramid. Meanwhile, William Kent (1685–1748), a renowned architect and painter, was behind a massive change, doing away with the walls, hedges, and fences surrounding the grounds and opening them up to the broader landscape and horizon, thereby turning the whole of nature into a garden.

Designed by a painter, gardens become paintings, reproducing, with temples, bridges, and ponds, the paradisiacal atmosphere of the works of Nicolas Poussin or Claude Lorrain.

Thus at Rousham Hall, **William Kent**, who was first to use the "serpentine line," replaced the straight avenues of the formal garden and the neatly drawn canals with meandering streams and winding paths. He turned the classical terraces into vast lawns, introducing clumps of trees planted in irregular shapes, and dotting his landscapes with numerous cascades, lakes, grottoes, and fake ruins.

Towards the middle of the century, the garden held to be the most remarkable was the one at Stowe, near Buckingham, where Kent had designed some irregularly shaped lakes. But the man who drew up the final plan was the great **"Capability" Brown** (1715–1783)—the soubriquet came from his skill in highlighting a landscape's "capabilities" (his word). In his trademark style, recognizable in all the parks developed or restored under his supervision (notably Warwick, Longleat, Chatsworth, Blenheim, and Wimpole Hall), Brown would plant trees in round clumps, create meandering streams and large smooth lawns undulating up to the stately homes, along with a tree-lined avenue right round the property. For Capability Brown, the art of the garden was a way of sublimating the landscape. Nearly all the great gardens of the day—he had over a hundred to his name—were either designed by him or bore his touch.

He did not exercise his talents on the grounds of Stourhead, although it stands out as one of the really outstanding gardens of the time. It was designed around a large lake in the years 1741 to 1780 by the property's

owner, Henry Hoare II. Conceived in the same spirit as Stowe, these grounds comprise the same scenery of bridges, grottoes, temples, cascades, and other manmade features, making a stroll around this place and its gentle hills, planted with exceptional trees, absolutely enchanting.

The archetype of the eighteenth-century English garden, that idealized landscape, seen as a "living painting," looks like a stage set, where every nook and cranny holds surprises and picturesque views for the visitor.

What makes the English garden different is that it is the outcome of both a conceptualized vision and of complete control of the technical data. Seemingly unbridled vegetation develops at nature's own pace and is

The archetypal English garden, Stourhead, where the hills and follies hidden by the lakeside offer the visitor an unforgettable walk in Wiltshire.

transformed, depending on the time of year or the time of day. Unlike the French garden, the purpose of the English garden is to copy nature, not to dominate it, and it is wont to leave an impression of disorder, giving the imagination free rein.

The rejection of symmetry appears as a symbol of freedom, in direct contrast to the "straitjacket" of the formal garden. What was being sought was the balance of volumes, the harmony of colors, and the diversity of plant textures.

English gardens came in for aesthetic evolution throughout the eighteenth and later the nineteenth century. The "idyllic garden," the "sublime garden," and the "picturesque garden" in turn ended up influencing gardens on the continent.

Who is following on from this great art? Do British landscape architects still play around with these rules of naturalness and irregularity? A few major figures have marked the twentieth century, and others are coming to the fore today in a scene brimming with talent.

In the nineteenth century and the early twentieth century, the English garden saw new aesthetic developments, under the influence of some outstanding personalities like **Gertrude Jekyll** (1843–1932). A gifted writer, photographer, painter, and designer, Gertrude Jekyll turned the garden into a place of artistic experimentation, introducing sumptuous swathes of color in her famous "mixed borders," a combination of annuals and perennials. The creator of over four hundred gardens in Britain, France (Bois des Moutiers) and the United States, this artist, influenced by the Art and Crafts movement, composed some extraordinary scenes, combining with peerless virtuosity climbing plants, perennials, and rose bushes, and playing subtly on the balance of colors, scents, and plant textures. "Nature is such a subtle chemist that one never knows what she is about, or what surprises she may have in store for us," the great gardener observed.

Harmonies of colors and characteristic flower beds in a private English garden.

Another major personality was **Victoria Mary Sackville-West** (1892–1962), better known as Vita Sackville-West, who also played around with the irregularity and poetic profusion of the English garden. A novelist, essayist, poet, translator, and gardener, very close to Virginia Woolf, this larger-than-life character played a key role in the creation of her wonderful garden at Sissinghurst. Known for its famous White Garden, and also for the enchanting poetry and the profusion of plant life in all her garden rooms, whether it be the cottage garden, the herb garden, or the unlikely sounding Thyme Lawn, Sissinghurst remains an unforgettable garden.

Christopher Lloyd (1922–2006), for his part, belongs to the tradition of the gentleman gardener. The most remarkable part of his work is in his own garden: Great Dixter, a property restored in 1910 by the architect Edwin Lutyens. Great Dixter is an exceptional place, comprising a set of small gardens placed among some magnificent topiaries, a rose garden, and a vegetable garden, with a highly successful mix of flowers and vegetables, where Christopher Lloyd liked to create bold chromatic associations. There is also a large orchard, and teeming mixed borders, brimming all year round with annuals and perennials, as well as "wild flower meadows" linking up with the surrounding countryside.

Dan Pearson, educated at Wisley, worked at the Royal Botanic Garden in Edinburgh, where he looked after the Rock Garden, and the Royal Botanic Gardens (Kew Gardens), is part of an upcoming generation of British landscape architects. Indicative of the consideration he commands, he has already designed five gardens for the Chelsea Flower Show in London. He always begins with a deep meditation on the spirit of the place and works with nature, rather than trying to dominate it. He creates very dense and very sensitive gardens (witness his superb privately commissioned projects in Gloucestershire and Oxfordshire), always using carefully selected plants, which he knows how to match up with the soil and the location.

Subtle chromatic harmonies mixing grasses and echinaceas, created by Tom Stuart-Smith at Royal Horticultural Society Garden Wisley, Woking, United Kingdom.

Tom Stuart-Smith is another of the brilliant English landscape architects of the last few years. He has designed many public and private gardens, and as a worthy heir of the great colorists of the early twentieth century, he combines an outstanding sense of color with an amazing way with plants—this gives rise to gardens with great poetry, gardens like those at Wisley, Trentham, and Windsor Castle.

The scenes he composes with supple grasses, mixed in with colorful perennials and a subtle blend of box, dogwood, and echinaceas, are a paean to plants' freedom of movement.

One last great figure, who stands out through his ability to invent a whole world and tie in the garden and landscape with vaster historical or artistic issues is **Ian Hamilton Finlay** (1925–2006) with his amazing world of Little Sparta in Scotland, a philosopher's garden if ever there was one.

3

IF YOU LIKE . . .

ROMANTIC GARDENS

Are you, like Jean-Jacques Rousseau, one of those "solitary contemplatives who love to lose themselves altogether in the charms of nature ... which astonishes the senses and at the same time instills in the heart tender emotions and melancholy ideas"? Are you attracted to gardens for their "intimacy, spirituality, color, aspiring to the infinite," the distinguishing features of Romanticism according to Baudelaire? The romantic garden may be characterized by charm, poetry, and wistfulness, but many modern gardens are also endowed with these qualities. Abundant, luxuriant, with branches bowing under the weight of flowers, bushes, and shady groves, rich in vases and statues, the nature of the romantic garden is indeed to induce a dreamy state and "speak to the soul." It generally has winding paths and diaphanous outlines.

The archetype of the romantic garden, the **Ninfa Gardens**, located south of Rome, restored and created to look as they do today by the Gelasio Caetani family in the 1920s, lie in a unique setting: the ruins of a medieval village. In this sublime scenery, with its small bridges, architectural remains decorated with roses, and other colorful climbing plants dotted along a poetic walk at the water's edge, time seems to have come to a standstill. Overrun in spring by thousands of narcissi in flower, such a landscape cannot fail to move and give free rein to the imagination.

FACING PAGE

The Ninfa Gardens near Rome, combining ruins and arched bridges amid a very pure, verdant, and floral landscape, Cisterna di Latina, Italy.

Other gardens that can be classed as romantic are the gardens of the English landscape architect and publisher **Percy Cane** (1881–1976), most notably Dartington Hall, and Sulgrave Manor at Sutton Park in Britain, where the gentleness and delicacy of the scenery, in particular the poetic green velvet steps, allow visitors to escape and daydream to their hearts' content.

Meanwhile, the subtle ephemeral interventions of British artist **Chris Parsons**, on dewy lawns at dawn, create vast, fascinating geometric patterns on freshly mown grass, and are like romantic meditations on the beauty and transience of life. **Often bowing beneath the weight of roses, offering benches for meditation, and opening up vistas that stretch out toward infinity, generally speaking English gardens are an inducement to enter into communion with the landscape.**

DREAMLIKE GARDENS

Even a garden can immerse us in an oneiric atmosphere, carrying us off toward the strange, fascinating world described by Gérard de Nerval in the autobiographical *Aurélia* (1855), toward "those ivory or horned gates which separate us from the invisible world," and taking us to the moment when "a new light illumines and sets in motion ... odd apparitions." Certain gardens plunge us wide awake into a dreamlike state.

While some parks, with their mysterious charm, can themselves be the stage for fleeting visual hallucinations at particular times of day, certain scenes are deliberately intended by garden designers to take us to the fringes of reality and the imaginary. They offer us images with extraordinarily suggestive powers that, owing to their enigmatic character, are indelibly etched on the memory.

The gardens at Chaumont-sur-Loire often present scenes whose strange beauty strikes the imagination. These include the hanging greenhouse and the white chairs hovering on water by Christophe Marchalot and Félicia Fortuna; the unusual piano-without-a-player amid the poppies, from which Billie Holliday tunes would mysteriously escape, devised by the Dutch team of Strootman Landschapsarchitecten; the nesting-box museums of the visual artist Philippe Caillaud; the curled pieces of silver paper of Fabien Mauduit and Véronique Hours, all of which have the visitor utterly fascinated.

FACING PAGE
Birds' nest museums in the Métempsycose (Metempsychosis) garden at the Chaumont-sur-Loire International Garden Festival, 2010.

While the dream, as defined by Freud, is indeed "the realization of a desire," we doubtless find in these gardens a desire from time immemorial to walk on water, the state between two dreams in which sounds mix, with synesthetic effects harmoniously melding every sensation, and the desire for connection with loved ones who have gone forever.

Similarly, the unusual garden with colored paths by **Tori Winkler** (a private garden in Alexandria, Virginia) will set you daydreaming, with its strange purple and blue tones and the unreal apparition of a white horse.

Likewise, although their gardens are more artificial, the Swiss artists **Gerda Steiner and Jörg Lenzlinger** create an infinitely strange and poetic world, with thousands of imaginary flowers in suspension, like some supernatural garden in surrealist colors and shapes.

Such are the powers of suggestion of these gardens with a difference, with their invisible, secret, forever indecipherable richness, and the wealth of pictures that they conjure up abidingly in people's minds.

ECOLOGICAL GARDENS

Perhaps you are concerned about preserving your environment and biodiversity, and are more interested in experiments with ecological gardens, like those being conducted at the Jardin des Plantes in Paris, the Jardin Écologique in Lille, the Jardins Passagers (ecological gardens allowing public participation) at the Parc de la Villette, or by Gilles Clément in his garden in central France.

The ecological garden is an environmentally friendly garden that does not deplete the planet's resources. It includes areas left untended where natural species can grow without fertilizer, without plantings, and with no scrub clearance, making it an inviting spot for insects, birds, frogs, hedgehogs, and so on to come and feed or reproduce easily. The ecological garden is an asset to native plants, which are adapted to the soil's chemical condition and hydration levels, thereby obviating the need for too many pesticides and too much watering. It is a garden that diversifies species, accommodating larger numbers of living organisms, and so balancing predator and prey populations. It is a garden where crop rotation is practiced, enabling specific diseases to be eradicated. It is a garden where any scrub clearing is done mechanically rather than chemically. Lastly, it is a garden where composting is done.

FACING PAGE

The ecological garden can sometimes be a dry landscape garden, requiring no watering, as with these plantings by the British landscape architect Beth Chatto on the site of a former parking lot, Colchester, United Kingdom.

An adept of the ecological garden in his own garden in France, the landscape architect and botanist Gilles Clément advocates a management method that runs counter to the customary method of total control of the space by the gardener. For him, because the garden is "run through with living beings or agents of life, such as seeds and the wind, with their own different cycles and destinies," the related biological processes extend beyond its boundaries and are not limited to this enclosed private space. "Seeds come and go, carried by the wind, animals move around, continents drift, the environment is subjected to an infinite number of sometimes extremely rapid variations that are manifested even in the arrangement of private gardens." It is the Garden in Motion, which—with its spontaneous seedings, its wandering, invasive species—escapes the gardener's control, but which, to the gardener's delight, grows freely and haphazardly with its unexpected combinations, spontaneous grafts, seed transports, and extraordinary serendipitous surprises.

NATURALIST GARDENS

We are not talking here about the natural, ecological garden, but rather about gardens whose appearance and use of plants—grasses, for instance—and a degree of freedom in their overall design are inspired by nature, and although they may give the impression of being natural, they are actually perfectly controlled by the landscape architect's eye, expertise, and experience.

In the past, gardens used to seek to tame and perfectly order nature, carefully pruning plants that were often viewed as extensions of the architecture and transitioning out toward the untamed countryside. The increasing importance of ecology and also changing tastes have given rise to gardens offering a stylized version of nature, known as naturalist gardens, and they are very popular in northern countries, on both sides of the Atlantic and the English Channel.

Rather than offer a straight imitation of nature, some contemporary landscape architects prefer carefully arranged plant compositions that look pretty, and exhibit their idealized view of nature. Gardens of this type make use of wild or hybrid species in preference to plants drawn from conventional horticulture, the product of many years of selection that has taken them away from the lighter, chromatically more neutral appearance of the more natural kinds of plants.

The Dutch landscape architect **Piet Oudolf**, an outstanding colorist, for example, designs scenes of extraordinary fluidity, playing with the plants' colors, volumes, and growing patterns, and giving a natural look to gardens that in actual fact are elaborately constructed. The effects of rhythms and accumulations and the massive use of tall grasses give his gardens incomparable lightness, delicacy, and litheness.

Sylvie and Patrick Quibel's Jardin Plume (Feather Garden), in Normandy, is another example of these gardens full of grace and poetry, producing an impression of naturalness by mixing grasses undulating in the breeze and trimmed boxwood, annuals and perennials, golden ears, sage, and verbena, surrounding impeccable hedges—meadowland, of course, but meadowland wonderfully controlled by the talent of the garden's designers.

The main study and research center for this naturalist garden trend is at Sheffield University in Britain, which has on its teaching staff theoreticians like **Joel Kingsbury** and **James Hitchmough**, who invented the long-lasting flowering meadow concept. As pioneers, along with Piet Oudolf, in the use of naturalistic plantations that put on a lasting graphic show, these highly skilled experimenters offer an interesting alternative for gardens, in both aesthetic and economic terms.

FACING PAGE

Subtle combinations of grasses and perennials of which the Dutch landscape architect Piet Oudolf is an absolute virtuoso.

IF YOU LIKE . . . .

PHILOSOPHICAL GARDENS

A microcosm, an enclosed, protected space, the garden often serves as a retreat from the world in which to meditate, and provides the ideal spot for developing philosophical thought. After all, Plato and Epicurus chose to do their thinking in the garden, and artists and landscape architects are likewise drawn to this "science of the absolute."

Little Sparta is a perfect example of a philosophical garden. An extraordinary garden in Dunsyre, in the Pentland Hills—a landscape of desolate moors near Edinburgh—it was created in 1966 by the artist, publisher, and poet Ian Hamilton Finlay and his wife Sue Finlay.

This garden, which includes 275 artworks, is itself a work of art, a harmonious blend of poetry and philosophy, culture and horticulture. The garden was originally called Stonypath. Finlay picked the name Little Sparta in 1983, with reference to Edinburgh's nickname, "Athens of the North," thereby recalling the historic rivalry between Athens and Sparta. Finlay lived there until shortly before his death in 2006. This unusual spot, which blends in with the moors of the Scottish highlands, is thought to have been inspired by the garden at Ermenonville, with its monuments set as if facing the reveries of the solitary walker, the French eighteenth-century philosopher Jean-Jacques Rousseau. Little Sparta comprises several different gardens, designed in different years, and decorated with monuments, sculptures, and inscriptions inspired by antiquity, the French Revolution and World War II, taking the visitor through historical yet timeless worlds. Babbling brooks, fountains, lakes, and ponds accompany a walk full of surprises. Wandering down narrow paths,

FACING PAGE

A golden statue of Apollo, set in the undergrowth, like other works and stones engraved with aphorisms, which are dotted throughout a garden full of poetic surprises: Little Sparta, the garden of Ian Hamilton Finlay, Dunsyre, United Kingdom.

you gradually come to the Front Garden, the Roman Garden, Julie's Garden, the Temple Pool Garden, the Woodland Garden, the Wild Garden, and others. Everywhere among the stones, ruins, and undergrowth, sentences, aphorisms, messages, symbols, and poems lie among the heather, exuding an indefinable charm and mystery. Wandering around, you suddenly come upon strange sculptures, golden faces set in the greenery. Finlay's intentions are moral, philosophical, and poetic. He inscribes in stone and plant life his sometimes controversial and abstruse meditations on the way of the world and on Western civilization. According to Christophe Domino, Finlay, who followed an atypical career, saw the garden as "a natural extension of poetry."

As Ernest Renan wrote in *L'Avenir de la Science* (*The Future of Science*, 1890): "Philosophy is not a separate science; it is one side to all the sciences.... Philosophy is this common head, this central region of the great beam of human knowledge, where all the rays touch each other in a selfsame light.... The Ancients wonderfully understood this lofty and broad meaning of philosophy."

It is science that inspires the philosophical thinking of **Charles Jencks** in his outstanding Garden of Cosmic Speculation at Portrack House. This garden is an instance of philosophical reflection on where the world is headed and the advances of science in our time. The garden's architecture is intended to be symbolic, and even esoteric and cosmogonic, being a spatial rendering of the history of the advances of contemporary science.

As a broad-ranging reflection on the universe, the Portrack estate design is entirely based on mathematical chaos theory and fractal geometry. Charles Jencks's aim is of course to celebrate nature and the pleasure it gives us, but he takes the view that after all the discoveries made during the last century in biology, with the discovery of the role of DNA and its evolution, in cosmology or relating to the origin of the universe, our view and representation of nature can no longer remain the same. "There are plenty of new subjects for gardens." **Portrack proposes a profoundly original world made up of stairs, waves, and spiraling plants, symbolizing things like black holes and theories about the birth of the universe. Quirkily shaped hills and ponds, black-and-white checkerboard patterns, red colored bridges, shapes illustrating the equations of Planck and Einstein are dotted around this extremely undulating land, edged by a river, a bridge, and a railroad, which the landscape designer has factored in. This garden conveys the intuitions of science and philosophy through objects that we can understand, explains Jencks. We are living after Darwin, Freud, and Einstein, and we can no longer have a romantic view of nature.**

The Universe Cascade in Charles Jencks's garden, Portrack House (Scotland) United Kingdom.

Another contemporary philosophical garden is the **Site of Reversible Destiny— Yoro Park**, designed by the Japanese artist Shusaku Arakawa (1936–2010) and the American poet Madeline Gins, born in 1941. Since 1963, they have been conducting a visionary project, in the gray area between art and architecture. This park, created in Kyoto in 1995, came about through the idea of "making death illegal," for these two artists have "decided not to die." Their unusual garden, set in an odd crater, adorned with an assortment of buildings and steep paths, seeks to destabilize the visitor and "offer a new horizon" through a variety of physical and spiritual experiences. The site is planted with twenty-four different plant species and the inside of the main pavilion, called the Critical Resemblance House, is set out like a maze. In the midst of the hillocks and dips, nine pavilions with amazing structures propose unexpected challenges and experiments that are so many unanswered questions and inquiries.

PAGES 66–67
Site of Reversible Destiny, designed by Shusaku Arakawa and Madeline Gins, Kyoto, Japan.

IF YOU LIKE . . .

The Black Hole Terrace by Charles Jencks, Portrack House, near Dumfries, United Kingdom.

The autumnal
splendors of
the gardens at
Chaumont-sur-Loire.

A QUESTION OF TIME

PASSING TIME

VVhat better than a garden to give us an idea of the passage of time and the constant change affecting things? The garden is a paradoxical place vvhere time can linger or fly by, a place of transience linked to the infinite. Dormant shoots, buds bursting open, flovvers blossoming then slovvly vvilting, turning into fruit, fruit that vvill become seeds that fall and are reborn—these are the tangible signs of time going by. The changing colors of tree foliage, from tender green to dark green, then yellovv, purple, and suddenly black, reflect the passing of the days. The flovv of time is made visible through the garden and its changes. Its various cycles of life and death plunge us into rhythms that differ from those of humankind: infinitely shorter, infinitely slovver, and in all cases different.

While the rose "lived as roses live, the space of a morning," to quote the French poet François de Malherbe (1555–1628), oaks or cedars, a hundred or maybe a thousand years old, often look down at us from their lofty years, across the centuries, far beyond the human lifespan. The garden is indeed the mirror of passing time.

Time being, as Heidegger puts it, "the horizon for all conscious experience," the garden has a part in understanding the relativity of things. In this sense, constantly evolving, with rapid growth rates that will differ from species to species, it may be seen as an "open work," changing and susceptible to multiple interpretations and reinventions, according to the individual gardener's or visitor's imagination. Indeed, for Umberto Eco, an artwork must not be a motionless, static reality, but the opening of an infinite gathered into a form, which, as far as the garden is concerned, will take shape day in day out, year in year out. If it is true that, as Heraclitus (c. 540–480 BCE) claimed, "No man ever steps in the same river twice," nor can you ever walk in the same garden twice.

FACING PAGE
Jardin des Colombières, designed by Ferdinand Bac, restored by the French landscape architects Éric Ossart and Arnaud Maurières, Menton, France.

FROM THE EPHEMERAL
TO THE PERPETUAL

The permanent and the ephemeral, the long-lasting and the short-lived, perennials and annuals, evergreens and deciduous trees: these two opposing forces are constantly juxtaposed and intertwine in the garden. Michel Baridon sees this as the "great paradox": "each and every garden is a celebration of the ephemeral," and yet they all "triumph over time."

The garden may be seen as the place of perpetuity and of eternal renewal: the evergreen trees symbolize immeasurable time and a link between the earth and the sky; the hardwood trees, seemingly dead in winter, revive in the spring, representing rebirth. Yet the garden is also the home of ephemerality. Just think of the sudden, sumptuous magnificence of the Japanese cherry trees bowing under their extraordinary pale pink scented blossom, giving rise to joyful and yet wistful celebrations (*hanami*, or "flower viewing") of frail, fleeting bliss.

Delicate, slender, fleeting; some garden flowers will last for no more than a day. Thus, unlike the perennials, which survive through winter in the form of bulbs, tubers, or rhizomes, annuals like bellflowers, verbena, and poppies complete their life cycle in a matter of months or even weeks. They only pass through the winter period in the form of seeds.

Hence, many ephemeral garden layouts follow this logic, and feature numerous annuals, often to the displeasure of those who believe in the longevity of the garden, even though the ephemeral is in fact a central feature of any garden. This is no more than a temporary game, played with art and with time, using as materials plants that in any case would not survive through winter.

The Ephemeral Gardens at Chaumont-sur-Loire remain eternal through the memories etched in visitors' minds.

RIGHT

The Beauty Garden.

FACING PAGE

Laundry in Bloom, from the 2009 festival.

For Michel Tournier, "The ephemeral is not necessarily to be scoffed at." It offers people moments of grace and of the absolute, like those African prairies in Namaqualand that sprout up like magic for a few days in the desert after rainfall.

Land art is another form of ephemeral art, since it involves producing artworks with natural elements such as branches, flowers, and twigs, which are all perishable.

METEOROLOGICAL TIME

If there is one place where the role of the weather and the importance of the elements are crucial, it has to be the garden. When you live in the city, surrounded by buildings and stonework, you become oblivious to bad weather. But in the garden, the effects of sun and rain, storm and frost, drought and snow often have to be seen to be believed.

In this highly sensitive spot, plants react to the air, sky, wind, and temperature. Depending on whether the sun is weak, intense, or scorching, come hail, frost, or snow, the garden's weather-resistance will be an issue and the survival of its plants may hang in the balance.

But it is also very sensitive to light, which varies depending on the weather and the time of day. The garden is a living artwork, where the lighting and the scenery are constantly changing. Dawn and dusk, when the sun lies low in the sky, give the garden—like the most extraordinary movie lighting engineer—a truly moving beauty that gradually fades towards the hottest part of the day. The morning dew deposited on flowers adds a subtle poetry to plants, but snow, frost, rain, mist, and fog also have an incomparably magical effect on the garden. Nothing, for instance, is more enchanting than Piet Oudolf's meadows of grasses, caught in the frost and crystallized with hoar, or the boxwood in the gardens of Jacques Wirtz after a snowfall.

RIGHT

Subtle variations of light and mist, major components of the garden—here at Narborough Hall, Narborough, United Kingdom.

FACING PAGE

A mist-filled path.

THE ROLE OF THE SEASONS

The garden is without doubt the best place to witness the passing seasons, whether it be springtime renewal, the summer heat, the seasons of rain and mist, or the rigors of winter.

In spring, when the temperature grows milder, when the vegetation revives and turns green again, there appear "the wandering perfumes of the rising sap, the heady irradiations which float in shadow, the distant opening of nocturnal flowers, the complicity of little hidden nests, the murmurs of waters and of leaves, soft sighs rising from all things, the freshness, the warmth, and the mysterious awakening of April and May," as described by Victor Hugo in *The Man Who Laughs* (1869). This is the scented time of wisteria and roses, ash-blue paulownias, mauve and double lilac, and pink Judas trees. All gardens are able to play with this extraordinary flurry of nature.

Then comes the summer heat, to which the garden brings the coolness of its ponds and fountains, its welcome shade, and of course the splendor of its foliage and flowers.

The fall brings to the garden its shortening days, falling leaves, fog, and rain. After the explosion of golden, purple, and orange foliage, it is the time for sowing, and for harvesting the grapes.

The coldest of the four seasons of the year, often called the rainy season, brings wintry weather and strips the trees bare. The winter is a tough time for the garden, although all the while spring is secretly preparing itself. The garden recovers its basic outlines and the dead straight rows of box and holly are a wonder to behold at this time of year—just think of the gorgeous topiaries of Jacques Wirtz. As for the dry stalks of Piet Oudolf's grasses, they feature in some beautiful frost-bound scenes. The rigor of winter is a great attraction to some contemporary landscape architects, who are fond of clean lines and the graphic possibilities afforded by a total absence of leaves.

ABOVE
The snow-covered hills of Charles Jencks's Garden of Cosmic Speculation, Portrack House, near Dumfries, United Kingdom.

FACING PAGE
Grasses and dogwood in the Royal Horticultural Society Garden Wisley, designed by Tom Stuart-Smith, between the fall and winter, Woking, United Kingdom.

Way to the Hidden Garden, designed by Dani Karavan, Sapporo, Japan.

5

GARDENS & CO.

THE GARDEN AND CONTEMPORARY ART

Many contemporary artists have been tempted to use plant life as the raw material in their work. Whether connected or not to land art, they install temporary or permanent works in every kind of landscape, in order to enter into a dialogue with nature. Some, like Daniel Spoerri or Niki de Saint Phalle, go so far as to create an actual garden, the exploit of an entire lifetime.

LAND ART AND *ARTE POVERA*

Land art (aka earth art or earthworks) first came into being in the United States and Britain in the late 1960s, and was produced by artists who rejected the museum-studio-gallery circuit and the rules of the art market. They worked in the open air, and created some extremely poetical, ephemeral works in plains or deserts, taking photographs to preserve a record of them. One of land art's emblematic works is Robert Smithson's *Spiral Jetty*, a spectacular coiled earthwork pier extending from the shore of the Great Salt Lake in Utah, others being the works of Andy Goldsworthy, or Richard Long's lines of stones.

Arch by Andy Goldsworthy, Cairnhead, United Kingdom.

Although his works are often out in open country, in Scotland, Provence, or on the other side of the globe, where his follies are laid down in stone, brick, or branches, **Andy Goldsworthy** also designs works with materials such as flowers, tree leaves, ice and snow. "Each work grows, stays, decays—integral parts of a cycle which the photograph shows at its heights, marking the moment when the work is most alive. There is an intensity about a work at its peak that I hope is expressed in the image. Process and decay are implicit."

Viewing himself as an artist working "with and upon nature," **Nils-Udo** creates his *Paradise Garden* out of branches, twigs, flowers, and leaves that he picks up along the way, also immortalizing his frail and transient compositions through photography. A carver of instants of eternity, the author of scenes of absolute grace, he also creates powerful works full of vitality, like his giant nests that evolve over time.

And on altogether a different scale, how could we forget the spectacular installations of Jeanne-Claude and Christo, scattered around the world, and notably their intervention on the Surrounded Islands, near Miami, which they encircled, in 1983, with some huge fuchsia-pink belts, so as to form what looked like giant flowers in the blue

A transient installation by Nils-Udo: a delicate assemblage of dark leaves and petals floating on water.

vastness? Their sumptuous *Wrapped Trees* in Berower Park, near Basel, are another example of this approach, which "suspends the obviousness of the world."

Another movement dating from the 1970s, *arte povera* uses nature and the changes in nature as the subject matter of some infinitely poetic and fragile works.

A leading exponent of *arte povera*, the Italian artist **Giuseppe Penone**, searching for signs inscribed in the memory of vegetable and mineral materials, looks for traces of human presence and sensitivity, which he reveals and

delicately highlights in his secret gardens. Trees, imprints, bark, and other such things take us into the domain of the invisible. Central to a masterly and multiform work, *Il giardino delle sculture fluide* (The Garden of Fluid Sculptures, at the palace of Venaria Reale), a visit studded with these subtle gestures at every turn, is the most important installation that this immense artist has produced to date. Artists like **François Méchain, Dominique Bailly,** and **Bob Verschueren** also belong to this family, whose relationship with nature is the rationale for their art.

GARDENS AS A SOURCE OF INSPIRATION
While on the face of it practicing neither land art nor *arte povera*—or even art in nature—some artists will resort from time to time to nature as a source of inspiration.

For his transient work *A Forest of Lines*, produced at the Sydney Opera House in 2008, **Pierre Huyghe**, a French film- and video-maker, had more than a thousand trees installed in this vast concert hall, with all the seats removed, thereby creating a veritable tropical forest veiled in mist, in which visitors could lose their bearings. In this way, the artist plunged them, in a unique experience, into a fragile natural environment, an extraordinary and incredibly poetic garden-for-a-day.

Storm King Wavefield by Maya Lin: a wave of grass created near the University of Michigan, Ann Arbor, United States.

Meanwhile, **Dennis Oppenheim**, a creative artist who is difficult to pigeonhole, was close to land art for a time. The author of many unlikely fantasy pieces of architecture, in one of his projects he mercilessly sends up the *jardin à la française* by associating it with giant pastries placed on a tapestry woven out of grasses and brightly colored pigments.

One leading contemporary artist, Mumbai-born **Anish Kapoor**, who has lived in London since the early 1970s, created a bold installation in Kensington Gardens in 2010, *Turning the World Upside Down*. His huge curved mirrors—in which skies, lakes, and trees were reflected in amazing green or gray distortions—encouraged the visitor, unsettled by these weird deforming devices, to start wondering about the landscape and the environment.

The Chinese–American artist **Maya Lin** plays with vegetation over a longer time period. Her work on nature and the landscape "originates from a simple desire to make people aware of their surroundings." *The Wavefield*, a beguiling wave of grass that she produced in 1995 for the University of Michigan, is designed as a singular undulating landscape that obeys the laws of physics.

The author of numerous peace memorials, **Dani Karavan** designed a very graphic *Way to the Hidden Garden* (1992–99), a winding path of water, light, grass, and white stone at the Sapporo Art Park, on Japan's Hokkaido Island.

Meanwhile, the *Irish Sky Garden*, by the American artist **James Turrell**, is a strange, fascinating site built on Liss Ard, a hill in Ireland; it is a mysterious crater designed as a journey of initiation, an artistic quest in the heart of nature, akin to a tumulus, a pyramid, and a "celestial wall" with which to find the "inner light."

The author of numerous artworks relating to nature, **Fabrice Hyber**, whose trademark is the color green, in 2000 had 200 fruit trees planted in Cahors with their blossoming and harvest dates marked in front of them. *Les Culbutos* (The Toy Punching Bags), a project for the Loire estuary at Nantes in 2006, are also drawn from a "gardener's experience," with the—mobile—trees being tilted in various different directions. He designed his 2008 exhibition at the contemporary art museum in Tokyo in the form of vegetable gardens installed inside the museum and in various places around the city. "Art is born from thought, from the seed of thought, forests come from seeds sown in the soil.... I will sow ideas the way I have seeded the forest."

Among the very contemporary variations, we must not forget the recent work by **Jorge Macchi**, presented as part of the 2011 Lyon Biennale of Contemporary Art on some wasteland at Vaulx-en-Velin: the reconstruction of a fragment of a formal garden, inspired by the one in Alain Resnais' movie *Last Year at Marienbad*.

The Falling Garden, designed by Jörg Lenzinger and Gerda Steiner, Venice Biennale, 2003.

ARTISTS' GARDENS

The taste for gardens can lead artists into major experiments that engage their art and lives in profound ways.

Thus the Tuscany garden of **Daniel Spoerri** (born 1930), who, not content just to install his own works—stone mazes and bronze unicorns—on his 39-acre (16-hectare) estate, also includes over a hundred sculptures by Tinguely, Arman, Olivier Estoppey, and others, all related to the fields, the olive trees, or the countryside generally. Each artwork in this extraordinarily wild and remote park is in dialogue with the elements and the soul of the place.

Another artist's garden, inspired by Antoni Gaudi's work or by Bomarzo's Park of Monsters, is the **Tarot Garden** of **Niki de Saint Phalle** (1930–2002), also in Tuscany, with its extraordinary building-cum-sculptures covered with polychrome ceramics, mosaic mirrors, and precious colored glass. With these "coves of tranquility" and fountains amid the olive trees and cypresses, the garden, a veritable paean to life, sublimates and transfigures the gentle landscape in this part of Maremma. "I know that this is what I am born to do, that I was meant to do; I was meant to do a garden that would bring joy, where people could bring their children, where they could meditate," says Niki de Saint Phalle. Giant dolls, fairytale animals, forests of mirrors, the tree of life and so on, in bright, luminous colors, drawn from the hyperactive imagination of an exceptional artist, make the Tarot Garden an utterly unforgettable "little garden of Eden in which man and nature meet."

A similar approach is taken at the Osun-Osogbo **Sacred Grove** in Nigeria. The Austrian artist **Susanne Wenger** (1916–2009) had been living in Nigeria since the 1950s after being initiated into the Yoruba mystery cult; she devoted her life to restoring and creating—with local artists—temples and sculptures for this plant sanctuary. These works in metal, wood, and clay are now part of a UNESCO World Heritage Site, forming an amazing combination, in this primary rainforest, of a European view of contemporary art and African artistic traditions.

Sculpture in the Osun-Osogbo Sacred Grove, Nigeria.

The **Rock Garden** of Chandigarh in India is the outcome of an extraordinary adventure—that of a self-taught artist, **Nek Chand**, who has created a world out of pieces of rock, ending up with a 39-acre (16-hectare) garden populated with 25,000 strange statues of people and animals, which has been open to the public since 1976. The "kingdom of gods and goddesses," a veritable silent army drawn from his boundless imagination, these fascinating, colorful characters made out of salvaged waste materials—ceramics, pottery, broken glass, fabric modeled with clay, among other things—populate a world of shady hills, adorned with some refreshing fountains and waterfalls.

Sculptures in the Chandigarh Rock Garden, India.

COLLECTORS' GARDENS

Collectors, too, create gardens that are out of the ordinary. As major experimental collections in gardens and in places linking art with plant life, Inhotim in Brazil and LongHouse Reserve in the United States are interesting examples of personal commitment to art in gardens.

Founded in the 1980s by the steel tycoon Bernardo Paz, **Inhotim**, located 40 miles (60 kilometers) outside Belo Horizonte, is both the largest botanical garden in Brazil and the largest open-air museum in Latin America. Covering nearly 124 acres (50 hectares), this extraordinary park is home to a wide range of botanical species (over 4,700), with landscaping done in 1994 under the aegis of Roberto Burle Marx. It now contains over five hundred artworks by more than a thousand artists from over thirty different countries.

An amazing symbiosis between exuberant tropical vegetation and the last word in contemporary art, this garden, which holds the world's biggest collection of palm trees and the work of artists including Giuseppe Penone, Ernesto Neto, and Dominique Gonzalez-Foerster, is the scene of an exceptional dialogue between art and nature.

The gardens of **LongHouse Reserve**, another amazing venue, accommodate every form of art, echoing the aesthetic and spiritual concerns of its founder, the world-renowned textile designer Jack Lenor Larsen. This estate in East Hampton, near New York, showcases works by many of the leading contemporary sculptors, offering visitors some inspired settings closely linking art and plant life.

Another venue that should be mentioned here is the **Kröller-Müller** museum (13,590 acres/5,500 hectares) a gift to the Dutch state in 1938, the brainchild of a collector, a woman who wanted to set up a "museum house" comprising close on twelve thousand artworks in the middle of the De Hoge Veluwe national park, near the German border. The sculpture garden, one of Europe's biggest, is beautifully set amid harmonious plantings of oak trees and heather. Another collector's dream, on a different scale, is the **Donjon de Vez** castle keep, not far from Compiègne, France. This belongs to the auctioneer Francis Briest, and is home to an art collection set off by the minimalist garden, which is designed by the landscape architect **Pascal Cribier** and inspired by medieval iconography, with

Rejecting historicism of any kind, Pascal Cribier plays with the codes of medieval imagery. In its disproportion, Jean-Pierre Raynaud's Golden Pot underlines the absence of scale while strollers (and lawn mowers) move among the tall stalks of Siberian irises.

its carpets of a thousand flowers and its remarkable foreshortening of perspective. The emblematic image of this inspired spot, a water mirror edged with blue irises, reflecting both the sky and the architecture, also reflects the golden light of a giant flowerpot by Jean-Pierre Raynaud.

At the Château de la Mormaire, France, the artworks of the great collector François Pinault interact magnificently with the garden designed by Louis Benech. Another collector's adventure is the dreamlike world being created (since 1995) by the "garden artist" Patricia Laigneau, at the Château du Rivau near Tours. Her Enchanted Forest and her Paradise Orchard offer a highly poetic setting to guest artists such as Philippe Ramette, Jean-Pierre Raynaud, and Fabien Verschaere.

THE GARDEN AND ARCHITECTURE

A slick double act

The architect and the landscape gardener form an impressive duo, often producing veritable masterpieces. An archetypal image of this fruitful interplay between the garden and architecture is provided by the Villa Noailles, in Hyères on the French Riviera. This Mecca of the Roaring Twenties, resonating to the sound of festivals and passionate intellectual debate, was designed for the Vicomte de Noailles by the architect Robert Mallet-Stevens. It stands on the hill of the old ruined castle overlooking the town and the villa has a large Mediterranean garden. But, most of all, it has an extraordinary cubist garden, designed in 1925 by the landscape architect Gabriel Guevrekian—a fascinating extension in red and blue geometrical figures, making subtle use of the vegetation.

Meanwhile, the gardens of the Brazilian landscape architect **Roberto Burle Marx** (1909–1994) have kept up an ongoing interaction with the architecture, whether it be though the artist's constant collaboration with the top architects of his day, or through the way he himself contrived to inscribe geometric shapes in the vegetation as much as in the stonework. Roberto Burle Marx shares Oscar Niemeyer's fondness for "free-flowing sensual curves," the breakup of symmetrical patterns, and the use of strict forms. Instantly recognizable, his famous colored roadways are emblematic of his style, illustrated by the Copacabana promenade in Rio de Janeiro, where the palm trees of the Avenida Atlântica are dotted along his gray and white Portuguese stone mosaics, forming a huge abstract canvas. Combining nature and architecture, this "painting," when viewed from the balconies of the bay hotels, offers a constantly changing landscape constructed by the landscape architect.

Cubist garden at the Villa Noailles, Hyères, France.

Another major figure in architecture and nature, this time European, is **Antoni Gaudi**. Whether it be the buildings or the gardens he designed, in Barcelona and elsewhere, the work of the great architect Antoni Gaudi (1852–1926) is also considerably influenced by the shapes of nature. The immense garden he designed in Parc Güell—with its round carved stones, wrought ironwork, and tree-shaped columns—bear the trace of this profound inspiration just as much as his brightly colored ceramics. His is original work, full of curves, which blends in with nature and reproduces it harmoniously; the overall visual effect is breathtaking. With its footbridges, steps, the hypostyle hall with a hundred columns dripping with water recovered from the feed tanks for the fountains, and paths leading to the world's longest undulating bench, the park is an unforgettable universe, combining a garden, architecture, and a surrealist world view.

Gaudi's architecture inspired the renowned German artist and architect **Friedensreich Hundertwasser** (1928–2000), famous for his generous use of colors, curves, and "wavy" walls. Fascinated by the organic profusion of forms, this unclassifiable artist is held to be one of the great pioneers of humanist ecological architecture. His Green Citadel in Magdeburg, his Waldspirale (Forest Spiral) in Darmstadt, Germany; and the undulating Hundertwasserhaus in Vienna, Austria, with a riot of bright colors and very luxuriant vegetation, are testimony to his irresistible love of nature and of gardens.

Hundertwasser haus, Waldspirale (Forest Spiral), Darmstadt, Germany.

GREEN ARCHITECTURE

No doubt many designers have been inspired by tales of the hanging gardens of Babylon, uniformly covered with greenery, their legendary terraces planted with trees and adorned with enchanting fountains. And the projects of Emilio Ambasz and Édouard François' "buildings that grow" are really a contemporary version of those fabulous gardens of antiquity. Illustrating the current trend of using vegetation for its aesthetic properties as much as for the freshness that it brings to our stifling urban worlds, these green buildings are in the vanguard of contemporary creative architecture—both for the plants they contain and the technical processes that they use, such as thermic glass, photovoltaic cells, mist spray systems, and phytopurification through plants. They are architects' answers to the fundamental questions being posed by societies deeply concerned about global warming.

Utopian architecture by Vincent Callebaut: project for The Perfumed Jungle, Hong Kong, China.

The vertical gardens of the architect and landscape designer, **Édouard François**, who was ahead of his time ecologically speaking with his Flower Tower, as he was with his Building that Grows in Montpellier or his bamboo building, are derived from this very "green" and very humanist view of architecture.

Also worthy of mention in this category is the extraordinary green pyramid, overflowing with exuberant gardens, designed by the Argentinian architect **Emilio Ambasz** in Fukuoka, Japan.

We think too of the spectacular architecture buried under a garden of the Nanyang Technological University in Singapore. The building's roof, with its stories and offices out of sight, rolls out into the city like an impeccable and fascinating green ribbon.

Architecture, which is often imposing because of its triumphant verticality, can—on occasion—slip humbly underground. For a project for the Ewha Women's University in Seoul (2008), where 22,000 female students are in residence, the architect **Dominique Perrault** contrived to dig a gigantic furrow, a deep gash surmounted by a garden on the roof, thus reconstructing a landscape previously left derelict, and recovering links with the lost footpaths of a large park. With this extraordinary glass and metal building buried under a garden, he thus establishes—re-establishes—a physical, sensory, and landscape relationship between the university and the city.

It is hard to quote them all, but the magnificent vertical garden at the Musée des Arts Premiers, on Quai Branly in Paris, the green roof by **Renzo Piano** at the California Academy of Sciences, Daniel Libeskind's green skyscrapers, the deliriously fascinating projects by Minsuk Cho of Mass Studies, or by Vincent Callebaut for Hong Kong, proceed from this same determination to put nature back into the heart of the city and the garden as close to the residents as possible.

Édouard François' Flower Tower with its bamboo facades, Asnières, France.

COLOR ABOVE ALL ELSE

Architecture and color interact magnificently with plant life. Color is central to the work of Luis Barragán, a Mexican architect born in 1902, who had dreams of "gardening the architecture" and was forever playing with forms and with light. The daring chromatic harmonies of his projects were carefully controlled by this artist sensitive to every nuance and every detail. Color lends incredible beauty and extraordinary energy to his works, whether it be the Cuadra San Cristóbal property in Mexico City, or the symphony in mauve major with mauve paulownias on a fuchsia frontage, coupled with intense blue sky and pale pink low walls at Casa Gilardi, also in Mexico City.

The French architect **Bernard Tschumi**, born in 1944, also readily uses color in his architecture, notably the strength and flamboyance of red. His twenty-six red follies at the Parc de la Villette in Paris both give rhythm to the park and cheer it up with their bright color, the perfect counterpoint to the green of the trees and lawns.

The Japanese architect **Tadao Ando**, born in 1941, also makes full use of the powers of color and light. The Oval, located near the Benesse House Museum in Naoshima— a delicate building concealed beneath a garden—is a perfect example of his mastery of chromatic vibrations.

Fountains and colorful gardens at Cuadra San Cristóbal, Los Clubes, Mexico City, Mexico.

Red folly by Bernard Tschumi at the Parc de la Villette, Paris, France.

THE GARDEN AND DESIGN

Designers have green fingers, too. The spirit of the garden imbues design, and nature—in its every shape and form—remains a source of unbounded inspiration for producing everyday objects. All kinds of manipulations, appropriations, imitations, and hybridizations give rise to nevv forms connected to plant life, making this one of the most inventive trends in contemporary design today. Ceilings, vvalls, chandeliers, parasols, coatracks, carpets, chairs, or garden accessories: there is nothing that escapes the bubbling imagination of a generation inspired by greenery.

Exploring every potentiality of our relationship with the garden, the French designer **Patrick Nadeau** is helping to abolish the boundary betvveen indoors and outdoors. His is a very open approach, unhesitatingly combining natural and artificial materials. He surprises with his amazing kitchen garden totems, and his grassy coffee tables with the tabletop turned over; he enchants with his dreamy chandeliers, his leafy tables, and his box shelves groaning under the weight of plants.

His eccentric and poetic creations seek to integrate living things of every kind with great delicacy.

Alexis Tricoire, a French designer born in 1967, who has been marked by his childhood in Brazil and his discovery at a very young age of the magic of the tropical rainforest, has also produced many projects connected with plants. The author of some original botanical furniture, very early on he designed his Oreillerbes, grass-planted cushions, inviting the garden into the house; he also invents planted lamps and pendant lights. He grovvs some fascinating liana plants and makes subtle living teepees, with branches offering pleasant shelter.

Plant carpets by the designer Patrick Nadeau.

*Vegetal chair by
Ronan and Erwan
Bouroullec.*

Other leading personalities in contemporary green design are the two brothers **Ronan and Erwan Bouroullec**, with their Algues (Seaweed), which are light veils doubtless inspired by seaweed on the Brittany beaches of their childhood, and which possess an incomprehensible, irrational geometry. Flexible and spidery, they can be linked together into partitions. They reintroduce nature into cold contemporary interiors, "thus provoking their geometry, their whiteness, their uniformization, and their industry."

Another green invention by the Bouroullec brothers is their famous Vegetal chair, with its wonderfully organic lines. "The initial intuition was that of a chair which would sprout up like a plant. A plant-like chair, its branches gently curving to form the seat and back... The main issue was to follow the realistic geometry of a chair, while at the same time using the principles of plant-like branching as a construction model."

Green designers seem to be greatly inspired by chairs and armchairs. There is the Terra grass armchair devised by the **Nucleo** group of designers headed by Piergiorgio Robino; it is totally original, consisting of a cardboard structure filled with earth and seeds, which turns into a real grass armchair. Better-integrated furniture would be hard to imagine.

Neither the inventive Franco-Argentinian designer **Pablo Reinoso**, with his fantastic Spaghetti Benches and his extravagant garden tools, nor the eclectic **Matali Crasset**, with her Blobterre or her weeping willow house, are left behind in the green rage that seems to have taken over the design world.

ABOVE

*Tepee made
with greenery
by Alexis Tricoire.*

RIGHT

*Liana fork in
artist and
designer Pablo
Reinoso's
collection of
garden tools.*

Weeping willow
house designed
by Matali Crasset.

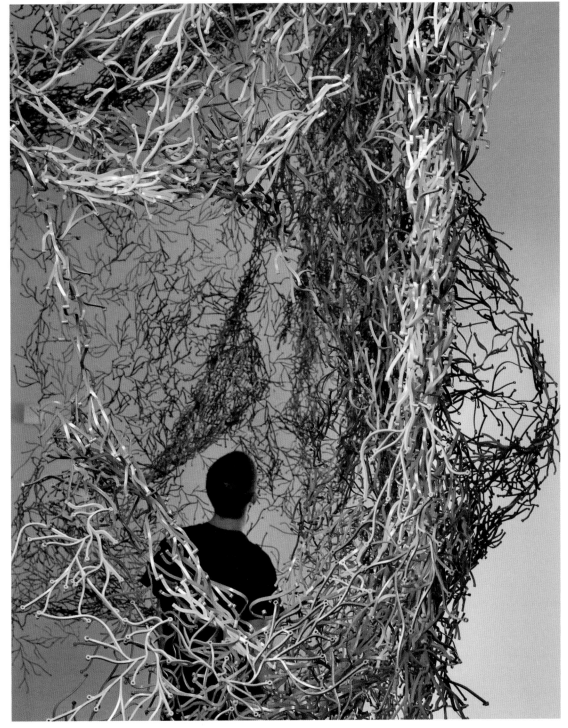

Algues (Seaweed), flexible partitions by Ronan and Erwan Bouroullec.

Hanging
Gardens of Colas,
designed by
Bernard Lassus,
Boulogne, France.

AN EXPERIENCE FOR ALL FIVE SENSES

A wonderful place for all kinds of sensations, the garden is truly the kingdom of the senses. It plunges you into a host of emotions affecting smell, sight, touch, taste, and hearing. The multitude of scents, sights, savors, flavors, feels, and sounds invite you to travel in time and space, and take you on a voyage through your memories.

COLOR

"Men seek light in a fragile garden with shimmering colors," wrote poet Jean Tardieu. Whether color is seen in philosophical, symbolic, or scientific terms, it is an element that no garden can go without. On the contrary, the garden exhibits fiery color, passing cheerfully from high-spirited monochromes to the subtlest gradations, playing magnificently with the light.

The Majorelle Garden in Marrakech, created in 1937 by the painter **Jacques Majorelle** (1886–1962), openly advertises the taste for color. To this day, the artist's villa deploys dazzling tones on the walls, with the dominant color an incredibly bold blue, as part of a living artwork, laden with jasmine and bougainvillea in a very verdant setting of palm trees, bamboos, and cacti of every kind. Sumptuous reds and tender pinks, punctuated by the polychromy of yellow, orange, and jade green ceramic jars, form an unreal atmosphere alongside magical fountains and colorful basins.

The Mexican architect **Luis Barragán** also shows consummate skills in combining the powers of plants and color. The mixture of orange and fuchsia at the Casa Galvez, of old pink and rust at the Cuadra San Cristóbal, and of mauve and pink at the Casa Gilardi show the extreme attention that the artist gave to color; so audacious, and unforgettably stunning in the Mexican sunlight.

The American landscape designer **Martha Schwartz** understood very early on how interesting, powerful, and effective color can be, even when it is not directly attributed to a plant. Indeed her first garden, a daring combination of green and purple, caused a furor at the time. Her garish green and plastic topiaries in the Splice Garden (Cambridge, Massachusetts), the Jacob Javits Plaza in New York (1996), and her red squares, such as Grand Canal Square in Dublin (2007), definitely possess a hypnotic power, although

The colors of an English garden.

very often the artificial comes first and the natural second. The same goes for the Hanging Gardens of Colas by the French landscape architect **Bernard Lassus**—fascinating landscapes of colored metal.

At the other end of the spectrum, and in a strictly vegetal register, it is with very great subtlety that a landscape architect like **Piet Oudolf** composes his plantations. He uses delicate palettes of color, working like a painter to design vibrant pictures sensitive to every shade of light. Whether it be in his own

*Voir Rouge
(Seeing Red)
garden,
Chaumont-
sur-Loire
International
Garden Festival,
2009.*

garden in the Netherlands, or Chicago's Millennium Park or the High Line in New York City, he uses his outstanding talent to combine plum, mauve, and pink perennials with huge inflorescences of beige grasses, playing with remarkable virtuosity on all the potentialities of the chromatic scale.

The top British landscape designer **Tom Stuart-Smith** also composes infinitely elegant gardens in tints so gentle and refined—just think of his pale blue or pink monochromes—that show his amazing pictorial sensitivity and knowledge.

The Red Sand Garden in the heart of the Cranbourne Botanic Gardens near Melbourne, Australia, displays an admirable combination of gold and red, and makes use of every shade of ocher and purple. Landscape designers **Taylor Cullity Lethlean** and **Paul Thompson** have contrived to produce some highly graphic scenery, playing as much with the different sand colors as with those of desert rocks and wild flowers.

The gardens of **LongHouse Reserve** (East Hampton, New York), created by the fashion designer Jack Lenor Larsen, also come with brightly colored works whose singular beauty becomes etched in the memory, like the blue garden, Cobalt Blue Reeds, by the decorator Dale Chihuly. The same holds for the creations at the International Garden Festival at Chaumont-sur-Loire, such as Voir Rouge (Seeing Red), produced in 2009 by the group La Superstructure.

Let us not forget the magic of light, which glorifies gardens and lends them a truly dreamlike dimension, giving rise in the evening to unsuspected harmonies and contrasts, whose qualities and energy definitely have a positive effect on the senses and on the mind.

101

Majorelle Garden, Marrakech, Morocco.

Cobalt Blue Reeds by Dale Chihuly, LongHouse Reserve, East Hampton, United States, 2000.

SCENTS

The sense of smell is also brought into play in contemporary gardens. The sweet, heady, fresh, green, or flowery scents of the garden can recall moments of inexpressible bliss. Who cannot bring to mind at least a few olfactory pleasures, caused by nothing more than a path edged by lilac, an arch of jasmine, or a honeysuckle bush? "Do you see, a perfume awakens thought," Victor Hugo wrote in *Les Rayons et les Ombres* (Beams and Shadows, 1840). Scent also rouses the senses and reminiscences. Perhaps souls gather their energy from this "luxury of the air," as Germaine de Staël so aptly put it.

Above and beyond the sensual euphoria that it produces, a smell carries within it buried worlds and takes us off into the domain of the inner self.

We of course think of the power of roses, of the bewitching charm of the rose gardens of Sissinghurst in Britain, Mainau on Lake Constance, La Châtonnière in the Loire valley, and that of the great creator of roses, André Ève in Pithiviers, not forgetting the Rose Cathedral in the Séricourt Gardens.

Stronger in the heat, scents are often the privilege of gardens in the south, full of tubers, lilies, myrtle, and wisteria. The output of the landscape designer **Jean Mus**, born in the

Heady scents from lemon trees and pittosporums in a private garden in the south of France.

capital of perfumes, Grasse, expresses the quintessence of the Mediterranean garden. To him we owe over a thousand gardens, including the Villa Fiorentina garden at Saint-Jean-Cap-Ferrat, designed not so long ago by the painter Ferdinand Bac. Rigorous and demanding, a perfect connoisseur of Mediterranean species, and sensitive to the spirit of the places entrusted to him, there was no one quite like Jean Mus for creating a setting, with serene green atmospheres in which, under pine and olive trees, box, lavender, and santolinas would exhale wafts of scented breeze, smelling sweetly of every fragrance of the *garrigue*, a mixture of verbena and heliotrope.

Éric Ossart and **Arnaud Maurières**, French landscape architects who are now also giving Morocco and Mexico the benefit of their talent, have created some lavish gardens including the Paradise Garden in the department of Tarn, the Alchemist's Garden in Eygalières, the Colombières Garden, which they reinvented in Menton, and also their gardens at Taroudant, Morocco, where the olfactory dimension is again very much present in each case.

It's hard to imagine any better spiritual food on the path to the Hesperides than the scented vibrations of white roses and pittosporum?

Summer blooms of lavender, roses, and santolinas in a garden in the south of France.

SAVORS

The garden is also the place par excellence for savors and flavors—exquisite sensations produced jointly by the taste and smell of a fruit or vegetable. The contemporary garden is in step with this trend towards inspired and green food. In search of rare, top-quality vegetables, many chefs and cooks have enthusiastically turned to designing their own kitchen gardens.

This is the case with great creative people like **Michel Guérard**, whose Prés d'Eugénie restaurant in Eugénie-les-Bains, in the Bordeaux region of France, are surrounded by aromatic gardens and a poetic "herb convent." The chef of the three-star L'Arpège restaurant in Paris, **Alain Passard**, for whom, thanks to vegetables, "taste has moved onto a new register, and tastes have, too," has kitchen gardens in three different departments of northern France, in the Sarthe, Eure, and Manche, the purpose being to give his vegetables a real local tang. This is delivered by the sand in the Sarthe for carrots, asparagus, and leeks; by the clay in the Eure for celeriac and cabbage, and by the alluvial deposits in the Manche, which are just right for herbs and spices.

The fruit gardens of Laquenexy, near Metz, France.

The magnificent kitchen gardens and aromatic herb gardens of the Manoir aux Quat' Saisons near Oxford, England, where over ninety varieties of vegetable are grown for the chef **Raymond Blanc**, also meet this same desire to have top-quality vegetables to hand, amid the lavender, in a really beautiful garden.

The remarkable garden at the Château de Valmer, in the Loire valley near Tours, renovated ten years ago by the landscape architect and botanist **Alix de Saint Venant**, offers a feast for the eyes, nose, and taste buds, a foretaste of the rare flavors of old vegetables. Along the ancient walls stand espalier fruit trees with peaches, nectarines, apricots, figs, apples, and pears. Ripening in the "berry patch" are black currants, *casseilles* (a cross between a black currant and a gooseberry), red currants, and raspberries. Various condiments, aromatic plants, and old-fashioned vegetables such as tetragon (New Zealand spinach), cyperus, and yacón, and also some outstanding *Cucurbitaceae*, have made this new garden a savant's garden of savors.

Meanwhile, the fruit gardens of Laquenexy, in Lorraine, devised by the landscape architect **Pascal Garbe**, are a novel collection of gardens based on this notion of taste. These gardens—housing a "conservatory of fruit varieties," with over six hundred varieties of apple—offer a delicious mixture of flowers "you can eat," kitchen gardens, and orchards, with a new surprise at every turn.

Kitchen garden in Sylvie and Patrick Quibel's Jardin Plume, Azouville sur Ry, France.

RUSTLING NOISES AND SOUNDS

When it comes to sounds—rustles, whispers, swishes, murmurs—the garden, a traditionally peaceful and restful spot, is the perfect place to experience them. Nowhere else can we hear as clearly the melody of running water, the fervent gush of water fountains, or the gentle lapping of springs. Numerous other murmuring sounds can also be heard, such as the humming of bees, the chirping of birds, the gusts of the breeze, and the tinkle of raindrops.

The landscape designers of today make no mistake when, as worthy heirs of their elders, they happily use springs and fountains, which spill limpidly over stone and carve out the silence wonderfully.

The small rivulets from the springs of Little Sparta in Scotland, the "cascade of buckets" in the garden of **Michel Desvigne** and **Christine Dalnoky** at the Chaumont-sur-Loire International Garden Festival, or that of the Jardin des Paradis by **Éric Ossart** and **Arnaud Maurières**, let fall a thin, delicate trickle of water, drop by drop, magically amplifying the calm of the arbors.

The sublime water sprays in the Gardens of the Imagination at Terrasson in the Périgord area, sumptuously matching the landscape of the Vézère valley, and created in 1996 by the American landscape architect **Kathryn Gustafson**, plunge the visitor, through their song, into an extraordinary fascination with the sounds. Water fountains spill back onto the stone, cascades and water steps form a breathtakingly beautiful whole.

FACING PAGE

The fresh and melodious waterfall in the Gardens of the Imagination, designed by Kathryn Gustafson, Terrasson, France.

The cascade at the Parc Diderot just outside Paris, designed by the landscape architect **Allain Provost**, with eddies worthy of a mountain stream; the wall of water and the water ballets of the Parc André-Citroën, designed by the landscape architects **Gilles Clément** and **Allain Provost**; the Water Mirror on the Bordeaux dockside devised by **Michel Corajoud**: all share this same visual and musical magic, now facilitated by the use of some sophisticated computer technology.

But it is not just the sound of water. Artists like **Erik Samakh** often work in parks and gardens by modeling and modulating sounds that play along with nature. Thus, the artist installed magical solar "fireflies" in the park in Chaumont-sur-Loire as well as suspending from the trees "sonorous flutes" that played with the wind, just as he did in Brazil, thereby creating a mysterious and poetic suspended presence.

The gentle trickling of the "cascade of buckets" in the Jardin des Paradis, by Éric Ossart and Arnaud Maurières, Gordes, France.

The euphonious sounds of the leaping water jets in the Gardens of the Imagination, designed by Kathryn Gustafson, Terrasson, France.

Path of topiaries
and Japanese
anemones
in a private
Mediterranean
garden designed
by Jean Mus.

7

PUBLIC PARKS & PRIVATE GARDENS

PUBLIC PARKS

The last thirty years have seen extraordinary advances in both public and private gardens, a trend that has been helped along by the talent of some bold and visionary landscape architects working towards these sweeping transformations. The newly awakened interest in environmental issues and the substantially increased urban population densities have led municipalities to take some major decisions to reintroduce green spaces into city centers. Important projects were commissioned in the 1980s for the purpose of redesigning public spaces and providing big cities with some "green lungs."

Thus in Paris, in 1982, the architect **Bernard Tschumi** constructed his scheme for the 136 acres (55 hectares) of the new **Parc de la Villette** around some spectacular contemporary red follies. Making sure to preserve the two main north–south, east–west axes, he also laid on a "kinematic promenade," opening onto theme gardens, including the Acrobatics Garden, the Bamboo Garden, the Sand Dune Garden, the Mirror Garden, and the Shadow Garden, along with two big meadows in the center.

The **Parc André-Citroën** (1986–92), on which **Allain Provost** and **Gilles Clément** worked together, and one of the major spaces that Paris has produced in recent times, offers a fine view of the Seine River, with its large central park (27 acres/11 hectares), its White Garden for walkers, brightened up with light-colored perennials, and its Black Garden, with its denser vegetation. The park also features Gilles Clément's *Jardin en Mouvement* (Garden in Motion), in constant flux, a Garden of Metamorphoses, some magnificent glasshouses, very fine sequoias, bald cypresses, and magnolias.

Still in Paris or the inner Paris area, noteworthy parks include the Parc Georges-Brassens, the Parc de La Courneuve, the Parc Diderot, and countless urban spaces created or being developed by great landscape architects like **Allain Provost, Michel Corajoud, Michel Desvigne,** and **Christine Dalnoky**.

We should also mention, among other remarkable achievements, the Atlantic Garden at the Gare Montparnasse rail station by **Michel and Christine Péna**, the large mall in the Parc des Lilas in Ivry-sur-Seine, the terraces of Nanterre, the Seine river banks, the Marne river banks by **Florence Mercier**, the Parc Clichy-Batignolles by **Jacqueline Osty**, and the Parc des Cormailles in Ivry-sur-Seine by **Henri Bava, Michel Hoessler,** and **Olivier Philippe** of the **TER** Agency.

Elsewhere in France, the Parc Saint-Pierre in Amiens by **Jacqueline Osty**, the Bordeaux botanical gardens by **Catherine Mosbach**, and the redesigning of the approaches to the Pont du Gard Roman aqueduct in Provence by **Laure Quoniam** are further instances of the high quality of these contemporary creations funded by public commissions.

Cascade in the Parc Diderot, designed by Allain Provost, La Défense, France.

Sporting events of global importance can also have some very positive effects on the urban landscape.

In Barcelona, the 1992 Olympic Games led to the creation of a number of public parks and walks, and returned to the local people spaces that had long been lost to them. Likewise in London, coinciding with the 2012 Olympics, "London's Pleasure Gardens" have added 650,000 square feet (60,000 square meters) of new gardens, to give the city some extra breathing space.

Reconversion of industrial wasteland, whether disused factories or quarries, has been another opportunity for building many new parks across Europe.

The remarkable rehabilitation of the Emscher Park steelworks in Duisburg, in the Ruhr area of Germany, by the landscape architect **Peter Latz**, born in 1939, with its gardens planted both inside and around the ruins of the steel mill, has become the last word in such "renatured" sites. The aspen wood planted by **Gilles Clément** on the roof of the submarine base in Saint-Nazaire (2009–11) is further evidence of this desire to reclaim natural spaces.

Old disused railroad tracks are another excuse for creating urban parks of a new kind, especially for pedestrian traffic.

The Promenade Plantée (Tree-Lined Walkway), in Paris's twelfth arrondissement (1988–2000), a wonderful flow of green in the heart of the city, was designed by the architect **Philippe Matthieux** and the landscape architect **Jacques Vergely**. New York City's remarkable High Line overhead gardens, designed by **Piet Oudolf** and opened in 2009, were inspired by the Paris walkway.

Tropical garden in Atocha Station, Madrid, Spain.

The development of riverbanks is also a key landscaping issue, whether in London (the Thames Path on both banks of the Thames) or New York City (Hudson River Park).

Large-scale projects entrusted in Bordeaux to **Michel Corajoud**, in Lyons to **Michel Desvigne**, and in Nantes to **Alexandre Chemetoff** are testimony to the importance of this issue of revitalizing these public spaces with a difference.

And if you walk through Madrid's Atocha Station, you will observe how even a railroad station can be turned into a garden.

Emscher Park, designed by the German landscape architect Peter Latz, in the shadow of the Ruhr steelworks,
Duisbourg, Germany.

PRIVATE GARDENS

Alongside these huge public works projects, cities are also being endowed with smaller yet poetic islands of preserved greenery, thanks to the talent of some inspired landscape architects. And the countryside has not been neglected either, with provincial gardens being built, year after year, by demanding designers according to their clients' special requirements, resulting in many unique creations.

Small urban gardens are an extremely useful laboratory for creating contemporary gardens. Thus the achievements of Camille Muller or Laure Quoniam, Éric Ossart, and Arnaud Maurières' Hanging Gardens, or the New York City gardens captured by the American photographer Alex MacLean—all evidence this taste for a green retreat in the heart of our big cities.

Despite wind, pollution, too much sunlight, and other difficult conditions encountered in cities, the talented French landscape architect **Camille Muller**, who used to work with Gilles Clément, certainly knows how to bring gardens to life by transforming them into extraordinary spots, importing ferns, vines, ivy, and wild grasses onto the rooftops; he tames the plantings while at the same time turning them into unlikely exuberant jungles. Interior patios and courtyards inside high walls become real urban paradises in which elder, hazel, convolvulus, and clematis vie in vitality to get us away from the hum of the city.

Inspired by the great American prairies, the landscape designers **Éric Ossart** and **Arnaud Maurières** boldly planted grasses on the Paris rooftops, although lightly enough not to block the breathtaking views of the city (Tilsitt, 2004). They also dared to turn their urban gardens into veritable zoological gardens (Rochechouart, 2001), with an abundance of palm trees and Mediterranean species.

Similarly, the private gardens of the French landscape designer **Laure Quoniam**, often done in white and silver tones, like Jean-Paul Goude's garden, show both great refinement and extreme rigorousness.

As for the countryside, there is plenty happening there, too, with work by landscape architects like Erwan Tymen or Jean Mus. A landscape designer from Brittany, Erwan Tymen can read nature like a book, and from this observation he derives all kinds of features to work upon, like a visual artist with an exceptional mastery of plants. More than a creator of gardens, he defines himself as an orchestral conductor whose role is to forge links between man and the potential of his natural setting. In his gardens, grasses take over from their wild cousins, heather copies moors, and carpeting plants cover rocks "in the same way as the wind would have sculpted them." He is the author of numerous seaside gardens in which clipped box, holly, and yew are mixed in with santolinas and delicately carved trees.

Landscape architect **Jean Mus**, for his part, is an expert in private gardens in southern France; he has work scattered around the Mediterranean rim and throughout the world. His green, scented microcosms express the quintessence of the charming plant life of such extra-privileged regions, with their abundance of intimate, secret gardens.

Play on sculpted curves in a private garden designed by Erwan Tymen, Brittany, France.

Wild grasses in abundance on the French capital's rooftops—a roof garden designed by Éric Ossart and Arnaud Maurières, Paris, France.

Limed trunks and dark greens in a private garden designed by Jean Mus reflecting the quintessence of Mediterranean nature.

Plant spiral
designed by
Patrick Blanc for
the stables in
Chaumont-sur-
Loire, France.

THEY DID IT FIRST

Technical transformations, breakavvay aesthetics, botanical innovations—you name it. Quite plainly, the last tvventy years have seen the garden emancipated, vvith numerous feats of inventiveness breaking completely nevv ground. Botanists, gardeners, and landscape designers are vying vvith each other to find novel vvays of reintroducing the garden into inner-city areas, vvorking differently vvith plant material and bringing our dreams into the heart of the garden. They are boldly trying out ever more creative designs, and pulling off all kinds of masterly surprises, performances, and reinterpretations.

THE NATURAL GARDEN OR "TAMED FALLOW LAND"

The natural garden is a total reevaluation of our traditional view of the garden. Leaving nature to its own devices, "to do as much as possible with, as little as possible against," giving power back to the plants, and just trying to help them along: this is the option taken by the landscape designer and botanist **Gilles Clément** in his luxuriant La Vallée garden where, since 1977, and off the beaten track, the gardener poet has been conducting an ecological adventure. His theories about the "garden in motion," and the rapid, spectacular movement of species, "which disappear as soon as their seeds are formed and reappear haphazardly," are drawn from observation of this natural garden. Here it is "the plant species that decide where they want to be…. This mindset leads the gardener to observe more and garden less."

These examples of "gardens in motion" draw their inspiration from fallow land, a living space in which species settle without "encountering the obstacles usually set up in order to shoehorn nature into tidy geometrical shapes," or meet aesthetic constraints. The seeds of the Jardins Passagers (Transient Gardens) at the Parc de la Villette sprouted in the aftermath of the Jardin Planétaire (Planetary Garden) exhibition. The gardener merely seeks to "tweak them so as to get the best out of them without affecting their richness."

VERTICAL GARDENS

The vertical garden is definitely one of the most spectacular new features to hit the gardening world in the last twenty years. This type of vertical garden was the brainchild of a brilliant botanist with green hair who, from a very early age, developed a passion for plants and their adaptability in primary rainforests. Deprived of light, they have to develop strategies for growth and survival. On discovering that plants do not need soil so much as a stable surface for their roots to latch onto, and a reserve of water and mineral salts with which to feed through photosynthesis, **Patrick Blanc** invented the vertical garden concept.

It was at Chaumont-sur-Loire in 1994, as a guest of the international garden festival, that the French botanist became a household name with his first vertical gardens. Since then, he has met with considerable success, installing nearly 300 living frescoes throughout the world, from Madrid to São Paulo and from Singapore to San Francisco. His vertiginous facade of the Musée des Arts Premiers on the Quai Branly in Paris, or his interior green wall at the Pershing Hall Hotel, also in Paris, feature among his finest works, and are a part of this veritable revolution in the way we look at plants.

Jardins Passagers (Transient Gardens), environmentally friendly gardens designed for public participation at the Parc de la Villette, Paris, France.

Vertical garden of the Musée du Quai Branly, designed by Patrick Blanc, Paris, France.

GREEN ROOFS

Not just walls but roofs are planted, too, bringing biodiversity downtown, with a whole host of advantages for the climate, air humidity, and health. Some northern countries like Germany, or Asian ones like Japan, are well advanced in this area, with their rooftops covered in sedum, wild marjoram, thyme, or wild thyme. These rooftop gardens, soothing embellishments of the urban landscape, have another advantage, as sound absorbers for noise abatement. This trend has now caught on with leading landscape and other architects, like **Renzo Piano**, who in 2008 covered the California Academy of Sciences in San Francisco with a green roof of undulating hills, as if wanting to slip the building "under the landscape," totally melting into it. According to Renzo Piano, "Architects have to know how to interpret the new developments of their day and keep up with the times. The museum is an interpretation of the ongoing green revolution."

The amazing Nanyang Technological University in Singapore is another example of the sudden craze for green roofs.

Impeccable and fascinating— the green belt on the roof of Nanyang Technological University in Singapore.

LUSH TOPIARIES

People have always enjoyed clipping and carving box, yew, hornbeam, and laurel into balls, cones, and pyramids, but no one before had thought of turning them into fascinating long waves. It took all the talent and botanical knowledge of the great Belgian landscape designer **Jacques Wirtz**, born in 1924, to introduce this movement and such unlikely curves into the architectural hedges of his many private and public projects, in a radical renewal of the art of contemporary topiary.

To push back the limits of what can be done with plants, and produce undulating shapes, the genius of clipped box, most notably responsible for the Jardin du Carrousel in Paris, would breathe new inspiration, flexibility, and great freedom into this timeless art, so as gently to reshape the way we look at the landscape. This aesthetic, graphic technique that the inimitable Wirtz raises to an art form has the advantage of playing wonderfully with light, tolerating the gardener's alterations and carving box as you would polish stone.

The green velvet of the topiaries in Jacques Wirtz's garden, Belgium.

TREE SCULPTURE

An inspired sculptor, **Marc Nucera**, born in 1966 and living in the south of France, is not a gardener, but a "sculptor of plant life," a revealer of new landscapes. As a specialist in trimming outstanding specimens—he operates on the rare trees in the garden at La Louve, near Avignon in Provence—he is extremely knowledgeable about how plants grow. He works on transforming tree silhouettes with matchless imagination and skill. He releases the forms buried in their branches, thereby creating new pathways through the landscape. What interests this amazing "landscape science researcher" is the densification of foliage. Far from freezing trees' natural tendencies, he follows them and creates unique works in tune with the spirit of the place, whose profound truth he uncovers: "It is all there, concealed; a kernel, an energy, multitudinous forms, a beating heart. It is rich, it is infinite. There is always a path to go down further, to encounter the unexpected, the unknown."

ABOVE

The fascinating silhouette of trees sculpted by Marc Nucera.

FIRE

The Czech landscape architect **Vladimir Sitta**, who is keen on the theater, has accustomed us to his bold stagings and his original use of materials, but here he is setting the garden ablaze. Paying tribute to the farming elements and traditions of the Aborigines, who are great users of fire to regenerate nature, the incandescent creations of this artist—who emigrated to Australia—elicit surprise and astonishment, as in this private garden in Sydney. These unexpected blazes are made possible through devices concealed beneath the vegetation, along with perfectly controlled technological sophistication.

RIGHT

Vladimir Sitta plays with fire in his experimental gardens, Sydney, Australia.

*Water Mirror,
designed by
the landscape
architect Michel
Corajoud, on
the quayside,
Bordeaux,
France.*

WATER MIRRORS

Not content to play with fire, today's landscape architects also contrive to amaze us with water, another familiar garden feature. The extraordinary Miroir d'Eau (Water Mirror) covering 150,000 square feet (14,000 square meters), devised on the Bordeaux quayside by the French landscape architect **Michel Corajoud**, is based on this magic enabled by new technologies, reflecting the sky, clouds, and architecture in a thin film of water. A fascinating and incredibly beautiful *mise en abyme*, this Water Mirror, which you can walk across, brings the infinite right into the city center.

MIST GARDENS

Like at the opera, where delicate smoke is sometimes produced to help the plot thicken or to guide—or mislead—the spectator's imagination, garden mists have dramatic powers which inventive contemporary landscape architects have clearly understood, people like **Vladimir Sitta** or **Peter Latz**, who produced an extraordinary, short-lived Nebelgarten (Fog Garden) at Chaumont-sur-Loire and recreated one in Munich for the 2005 Bundesgartenschau. With black Bavarian stones skillfully set in a spiral pattern, offering visitors views of the surrounding countryside, this garden plunged them into a dreamlike atmosphere, the thin water sprays playing with the light, the plant and mineral features, and creating all kinds of shadows and scintillations. **Kathryn Gustafson** has also used this type of device, to great poetic effect, in the Gardens of the Imagination in Terrasson.

PLANTLESS GARDENS

An iconoclastic muse of the conceptual garden, the American landscape designer **Martha Schwarz**, decided very early on, with her renowned Bagel Garden (1979), to operate counter to the conventional view of the garden; she also had the idea of completely eradicating plants from the garden. Disputing the artificial presence of trees and plants in the urban setting, preferring always green, immediately mature, and effective spaces, or ones decked with bright colors undamaged by the seasons, in an approach similar to the visual arts, she would scatter around city parks unusual materials and synthetic works that were remarkably effective visually. Thus the curved benches in the Jacob Javits Plaza, a public square in Lower Manhattan, add dynamism to the space with their bright color, and allow passersby to sit down for a moment in a cheerful atmosphere for all seasons.

Nebelgarten (Mist Garden) by Peter Latz, a subtle play of stones and mist.

Jacob Javits Plaza, designed by Martha Schwartz, New York, United States.

Topiaries in
Jacques Wirtz's
Belgian garden.

9

30 LANDSCAPE ARCHITECTS

EMILIO AMBASZ

Who is he?

An Argentinian architect and designer born in 1943, now living in the United States, Emilio Ambasz was a curator in the architecture department at the Museum of Modern Art in New York during the 1970s, teaching at Princeton and at the Hochschule für Gestaltung in Ulm. A great admirer of Luis Barragàn, Ambasz founded his own architecture agency, based in New York and Bologna, in 1976, and by 1978 was already making his mark with some surprising and original glasshouses at the San Antonio Botanical Garden in Texas. One of the core features of his work there is clear to see: the connection between architecture and the environment.

His work

Emilio Ambasz designs extraordinary gardens on buildings, growing an abundance of green layers on them worthy of the terraces of Babylon. The best example of this is the ACROS cultural exchange center in Fukuoka, Japan, designed as a completely green pyramid, with its 58,000 square feet (5,400 square meters) of greenery and its hanging gardens on fifteen levels.

Originally composed of 37,000 plants of 76 different varieties, the facade now contains 50,000 plants of 120 different varieties. Ambasz's aim is to obtain the triumph of "the green over the gray." The architecture disappears under this vertiginous vegetation. His motto, "100 percent garden, 100 percent house," plays upon this total osmosis between vegetable and mineral.

His philosophy

Emilio Ambasz plays on the aesthetic as well as the ecological effects of his constructions, which are completely concealed by the vegetation, with the positive effects that these large expanses of greenery have in bringing down the temperature and absorbing pollution. Viewed as the father of "sustainable construction," Ambasz is constantly devising new ways of introducing plant life into architecture. To create novel forms and new alliances leading to the melting of the mineral into nature and to the population's well-being, "to build with nature," develop an architecture both in phase with the environmental and social issues of our time, and fitting perfectly into the landscape: such is the creed of this passionate supporter of greenery in elevation, held to be one of the inventors of "green architecture."

Hanging gardens at the ACROS cultural center, Fukuoka, Japan.

LUIS BARRAGÁN

Who is he?

"What if instead of structuring the garden, we dreamt of gardening the structure?" This is doubtless the key aim behind the work of Luis Barragán. Born in Guadalajara in 1902, this self-taught architect, whose work was described by the landscape architect Emilio Ambasz as "autobiographical," died in Mexico City in 1988. Barragán trained as an engineer in Guadalajara (1920–25), working with builders at the same time. During a trip to Europe (1925–27), he visited San Gimignano, the Alhambra in Granada, and discovered the work of the great landscape designer Ferdinand Bac (1859–1952). Back home, he built housing in an eclectic "Hispano-Moorish" style, and also the Casa Luna and Casa Cristo in Guadalajara (1929). On another trip to France, in 1932, he met Ferdinand Bac and Le Corbusier. He settled down in Mexico in late 1935, where he built investment property and housing in the "international" style. In 1941, wearying of this soulless architecture, he decided to work just for himself and directed his business towards landscape design and urban development. In around 1945, he bought several hectares of volcanic land in the Pedregal de San Angel, which he transformed into a garden city conducive to meditation, as enjoying nature was a "sacred mission" for him.

His work

The building of his own studio-home at Tacubaya in 1947–48 marked the beginning of an extraordinary experiment whereby "the home and garden are one," the garden being a dual affair, "one part being planted out to accommodate trees and birds; the other, on the terrace, for the wind and clouds, a patio opening onto the sky, for meditating."

Influenced by Mathias Goeritz, a German sculptor based in Mexico, together they built the Torres de Satélite (Satellite City Towers, 1957), a landmark at the northern gateway out of Mexico City onto the Querétaro highway. He did three projects in the area, including the Fountain of the Trough (1958). One of his finest achievements was Gilardi House (1976) in Tacubaya, where, at the end of a corridor bathed in light, stands a magical red stone emerging magnificently from the water.

His philosophy

Sublimely colorful architectures, an almost mystical connection to the landscape, in-depth research into the pathways of light, and seeking well-being, spiritual elevation, and absolute harmony, Barragán's philosophy comes under what he called "emotional architecture." This concept, marking his refusal to reduce man to just his material dimension, took shape in 1940, when he decided to stop building dehumanized "machines for living in" and to create a garden on the outskirts of Mexico City. This place, first a maze, and then a library, was for him an experimental space that later became his own home.

Barragán's works are the fruit of a slow process, involving a lengthy survey of the site and understanding the genius loci, painstaking garden design relying on dialogue with its intended occupants, and seeing all the possibilities. The actual construction included constant spatial and chromatic adjustments, for the power of shapes and color was so fundamental to him. His main goal was to arouse emotion and stimulate creativeness in the person destined to embrace his spaces. "Houses, gardens, and fragments of landscape seek to offer man a territory of emotion and freedom where he can find himself and from which, cool, calm, and collected, he can step back and take in the chaos of the world." The house is part of the landscape; it melts into it and blends with it, and leads man to look upon it with new respect, and childlike wonderment. Barragán worked in an infinitely exacting and delicate way on the frail material of the human psyche.

San Cristóbal stables designed by Luis Barragán in Mexico City, Mexico.

LOUIS BENECH

Who is he?

Born in 1957 to an architect father and a mother with a passion for plants, Louis Benech is a landscape architect with an atypical career. He started studying law in Paris. After graduating, he eventually decided to follow his deeper passion and became a horticultural apprentice in England, with the renowned Hillier Nurseries. This immersion in one of Britain's great botanical locations enabled him to gain in-depth knowledge of plants and learn all the gardener's crafts and techniques, including everything there is to know about pruning, watering, potting, taking cuttings, and so on. Back in France to look after a private garden in the Eure department, with Pascal Cribier he won the competition to redevelop the Tuileries Gardens in 1990, which launched his career and enabled him to found his own landscaping agency.

His work

As a landscape architect in great demand, Louis Benech has over 250 finished projects under his belt in various parts of the globe. To him we owe, among other things, the development of the gardens of Château de Pange in the Moselle region of France, and a garden in the palm grove of Skoura, near Ouarzazate in Morocco. But he has also worked in Greece, Brazil, and New Zealand. Much sought-after in France, Benech has just created a landscaped walk in the gardens of the Archives de France in Paris, and was also involved in the Quai d'Orsay gardens and the Élysée gardens at Versailles. He did the Rose Garden for the priory of Saint-Michel in Normandy, and was responsible for the restoration of the Domaine de Chaumont-sur-Loire grounds, also designing the Parc des Prés-du-Goualoup (2012), a 25-acre (10-hectare) extension to the park where the international garden festival is held each year.

His philosophy

Convinced that his is "the finest profession in the world," working from his outstanding familiarity with plants, extensive knowledge of the history of gardens, and a sensitivity that allows him truly to understand both the locations and the expectations of the people who commission his works, Louis Benech also possesses remarkable foresight as to what subsequently becomes of the gardens entrusted to him.

When undertaking a project, he first takes a look at the garden's history. He highlights its strong points, studies the paths, the views, the relationship between space and material, the balance between empty and full areas. Having little time for fashions, he takes the long-term view: "You need to exercise common sense, modulate and nuance rather than do things because they are part of the zeitgeist." Environmental concerns led him to restrict garden maintenance and to work with native species and plants that require little watering. Benech does not see himself as an "artist." With supreme elegance and genuine humility, he just wants to bring "gentleness" and delicacy and to offer "places for respite from a world in which everything has been speeding up."

While he often works with affluent owners, this generous man "does not baulk at driving five hundred miles to answer a call from some garden fanatic with limited means, or to work for retirement homes, social housing companies, hospitals, or places where the garden helps to provide a living."

For Benech, the garden is "neither nature nor paradise." It is a place where he admits to often finding himself in a great state of serenity. "I am then overpowered by the beauty of the world, almost in a state of grace."

As he comments, "In the garden, there is something that participates in the wonderment at all Creation."

A private garden in France.

PATRICK BLANC

VVho is he?

A French botanist, Patrick Blanc was born in Paris on June 3, 1953. Even as a small child, he was fascinated by aquariums and tropical plants, and became a researcher with the French national research agency after studying natural science and writing a thesis on plants in tropical undergrowth. He has been traveling the world and primary forests since the age of twenty. He has also authored many scientific publications. A specialist of vertical gardening, Patrick Blanc does not see himself as a landscape designer, whose job he says is to work on man's horizontal path. For all that, he is one of the people who have done most to bring nature and landscape into our cities.

His vvork

Patrick Blanc is the inventor of the vertical garden. This original concept was inspired by his observation of nature. He saw that, particularly in tropical countries, nature takes root in the tiniest crannies in rocks, wherever it can find moisture. Considering how all the lost walls in cities—even the most barren ones—can be sublimated by such astoundingly beautiful green decors, his works have quickly spread worldwide.

1988: first vertical garden, at the Cité des Sciences et de l'Industrie, in Paris.

1994: Chaumont-sur-Loire International Garden Festival.

1996: glasshouse at the botanical gardens, Toulouse.

1998: vertical garden at the Cartier Foundation, in Paris.

2000: vertical garden at the aquarium in Genoa, Italy; vertical garden for the Forum Culturel Blanc-Mesnil, France.

2001: wall of the Pershing Hall Hotel in Paris.

2003: wall of the French Embassy in New Delhi.

2004: Musée du Quai Branly, in Paris.

2005: Avignon covered market; Square Vinet in Bordeaux (with Michel Desvigne); Astralia [sic], Cité de l'Espace, in Toulouse.

2006: the courtyard of 21 rue d'Alsace, Paris; wall in the Espace Weleda, eighth arrondissement, Paris.

2007: wall of the BHV Hommes store, fourth arrondissement, Paris; vertical garden CaixaForum, in Madrid.

2008: Musée d'Histoire Naturelle, Toulouse; arch of the Rond-Point du Grand Théâtre de Provence, Aix-en-Provence; Torre de Cristal, Madrid; vertical garden at the Galeries Lafayette, Berlin; Leamouth Development, London.

2010: greenhouse roof, Jardin des Plantes, Paris.

His philosophy

A discoverer of unknown plants and a great defender of the environment, this explorer of biodiversity with an ever-present smile and inextinguishable energy is a poet and artist at nature's service. Living happily among plants and animals, he is constantly seeking to share this passion. Believing that the planted wall beautifies the city as well as helps to reduce pollution, Patrick Blanc keeps recreating ecosystems on previously barren walls, bereft of life forms. Thanks to him, ferns, spiderwort, begonias, baby's tears, and other tropical species defy the laws of gravity and populate our towns and cities with these hanging gardens of a new kind.

CaixaForum, Madrid, Spain.

ROBERTO BURLE MARX

Who is he?

Roberto Burle Marx, who was born in São Paulo in 1909 and died in Rio de Janeiro in 1994, doubtless ranks among the very greatest landscape architects of our time, having designed over 2,000 public and private gardens. He was an artist, an architect, and a musician. Legend has it that his taste for plants and his early passion for landscaping came during a trip to Berlin in 1928–29, while he was studying painting and a regular visitor to the botanical gardens in Dahlem. There he is thought to have discovered the infinite wealth of flora in the country of his birth. On returning to Brazil in 1930, he began to plant around his house. Joining the national fine art college in Rio de Janeiro, he studied the visual arts under Leo Putz and Candido Portinari. In 1932, he designed his first landscape for a private residence designed by the architects Lucio Costa, to whom he was very close, and Gregori Warchavchik. He soon made the acquaintance of Oscar Niemeyer, working with him on a regular basis. From 1934 until 1937, he held the post of head of parks and gardens at Recife. This larger-than-life character was a regular participant on botanical expeditions into the Brazilian tropical rainforest, along with scientists, landscape designers, architects, and researchers hunting for plant specimens. In 1937, back in Rio de Janeiro, Burle Marx became Candido Portinari's assistant. He designed the first ecological park in Recife.

His work

His great public works include the Belo Horizonte Airport garden project, the landscape development of the Ibirapuera Park in São Paulo (1954), the landscaping project at the modern art museum in Rio de Janeiro, the landscape development scheme for the monumental thoroughfare of Brasilia, the Aterro do Flamengo landscape development in Rio de Janeiro, and the Parc del Este in Caracas. He is also the designer of the approaches to the fabled Copacabana beach, famous the world over for its promenade with its black and white paving stones in colorful waves running right along the seafront.

He undertook countless private projects. One of his last works was to help design the Inhotim Park in 1993. He had studied the plants on site with the botanist Henrique Lahmeyer de Barreto Mello. One of his life's great adventures would be the tropical plant collection he created at Guaratiba, south of Rio. This vast property, covering 89 acres (36 hectares), purchased in 1949, was bequeathed to the state in 1985 and listed as a national monument. Renamed Sitio Roberto Burle Marx, it now houses over 3,500 plant species. A fervent environmentalist, Burle Marx was also involved in protecting the tropical rainforest and combating the devastation caused by intensive farming practices.

His philosophy

When one looks at the plan of a Burle Marx garden, it is like looking at an abstract painting hanging on a wall. The architecture, pathways, interplay of colors between flower beds, water features, clumps of trees, and colorful patches of flowers are all plain to see. What makes his style so different is the organic and lyrical movement of shapes and volumes and the use of a chromatic range deeply in harmony with the Brazilian flora and landscape. His work is indeed characterized by the use of tropical vegetation and its luxuriance as a structural element in the overall landscape design.

The breaking up of symmetrical patterns in the design of his spaces is a constant feature, as is the utilization of monochrome flat tints, mosaics of colored stone on the ground, often black and white. Burle Marx had a fondness for winding shapes and for plants in checkerboard patterns.

A multitalented artist with extraordinary enthusiasm and generosity, as a creator and stage director in love with life, he was constantly reinventing the landscape and sculpting Brazilian nature, which remained for him the most fascinating material, behind many of his green masterpieces.

Checkerboard patterns, characteristic of Roberto Burle Marx's style, Tacaruna, Brazil.

FERNANDO CARUNCHO

Who is he?

Born in Madrid in 1957, Fernando Caruncho studied art and philosophy at the Universidad Autónoma de Madrid, before taking courses at the Castillo de Batres horticultural school. This dual education was to play a key role in the art of this very important Spanish landscape architect, who also has a passion for painting, notably that of the Italian Renaissance artists. "One of my main sources of inspiration is painting, especially that of the Trecento and the Quattrocento, Giotto's painting." He set up his own agency in 1979 and has already completed over two hundred projects in Spain, France, the United States, and Japan.

His work

Caruncho has designed a great many private gardens, most notably the Casa Caruncho, his own garden in Madrid, the Mas de les Voltes near Girona, designed in 1997, the Castel de Ampurdán in Catalonia, the Mas Floris in 1986, the Water-Lily Garden in S'Agaro on the Costa Brava in 1989, the Florida in Madrid in 1988, and the Pliny Garden in Majorca.

His philosophy

Simplicity, rigor, and a taste for geometry and symmetry characterize the very formal and very contemporary gardens of Fernando Caruncho, whose work synthesizes the core principles of order and balance inspired by ancient Greece and the history of the landscape. In particular, he is not insensitive to the green oases of the magnificent Arab-Andalusian gardens of his childhood. He has also always been keenly interested in irrigation science and the farming traditions of old, which he uses very intelligently in everything he does.

Water, light, and geometry play key roles in his work, which is instantly recognizable through his absolute sense of the use of space and the constant play between the garden and its outside surroundings, just as much as between the interior and the exterior in architecture. "My gardens are a succession of lights and shades," Caruncho stresses. "You pass from an opening to a closed section, then on to another opening, and so on." With a great fondness for contrasts, playing masterfully with the gold of the stone and the dark depth of the plants, he is bold enough to add wheat, whose blond color is an extraordinary contrast with the emerald of oak trees or the silver-gray of centuries-old olive trees. He also likes to draw scholarly square patterns of cypresses and orange trees, or to create luxuriant pergolas of wisteria, roses, and jasmine. Working on several levels, and playing all the time on the relationship between plant and mineral masses, with multiple water mirrors, he plants infinitely poetical scenes that are not without a certain dramatic quality. Stairs, colonnades, topiaries, and ponds on different levels all contribute to this timeless, philosophical atmosphere. He is mindful that Plato taught in a garden. His landscapes and gardens, places for reflection and meditation, are also designed to bring happiness and peacefulness. While Caruncho has a passion for philosophy, for him, "It is not the brain or reason that helps the hand, it is the hand that becomes independent, guided by the unconscious" in search of extreme beauty.

Cypresses, olive trees, and wheat mingle together at Mas de Les Voltes, Castel de Ampurdán, Spain.

ALEXANDRE CHEMETOFF

Who is he?

Born in 1950, Alexandre Chemetoff is an architect, urban planner, and landscape designer, and a graduate of the École Nationale Supérieure du Paysage (France's national college of landscape architecture) in Versailles. He founded the Bureau des Paysages in 1983, a landscape office composed of architects, landscape designers, and town planners. For designing gardens was not enough for the young landscape architect, who designed the Bamboo Garden in the Parc de la Villette. "When you are convinced that the territory forms a whole, you cannot be content with planting trees on your own little patch."

Since 2008 he has been running his own company, Alexandre Chemetoff 8 Associés, which carries out surveys and project-managing operations, illustrating his multidisciplinary approach, sometimes combining in a single project architecture, construction, urban planning, public spaces, and landscape, with "a concern for overall understanding of the phenomena that transform the territory": from the tiny detail to the large scale. Alexandre Chemetoff is very attached to this "polyculture." He was awarded the Grand Prix de l'Urbanisme (for urban planning) in 2000.

His work

Alexandre Chemetoff has completed many projects, including gardens, parks, and public spaces, such as the Bamboo Garden in the Parc de la Villette (1985–87), development of the banks of the River Meurthe at Nancy (1989–), development of the beach at Le Havre (1992–94), or the Parc Paul Mistral in Grenoble (2004–8).

He has undertaken urban projects like the design of Boulogne-Billancourt town center (1996–2001), transformation of the Île de Nantes island (2000–10), the Plateau de Haye in Nancy (2004–), and the Plaine Achille in Saint-Étienne (2009–).

He has also been involved in building projects, like the Deux Rives multipurpose building in Nancy (2002–8), the construction of a Paris housing block on the corner of Rue Bichat and Rue du Temple (2009–), and a garden city, La Rivière, in Blanquefort (2006–10). Cultural amenities projects include those at Vauhallan (2000–2), the Maison des Sports in La Courneuve (2004–6) or the Champs-de-Mars shopping mall in Angoulême (2003–7).

His philosophy

As an adept of a cross-disciplinary approach, Alexandre Chemetoff rejects any limits or boundaries between the landscape and architecture. He has opted to ply his trade "openly and freely." He sees practicing his profession as a "commitment in the world." "The program is a question raised, the site a place of resources, and the project a way of changing the rules of the game." Any transformation project, no matter how radical, has to be in relation to what already exists, which is not a constraint but, on the contrary, "a resource.... Familiarity with a spot means you have to practice it, experience it, and give yourself the space of the project as a time for possible discoveries." Whether he is combining concrete and vegetation in his Bamboo Garden at La Villette, a veritable "manifesto of leaves and cement," or rehabilitating areas set aside for leisure activities, like the beach at Le Havre, or passionately redesigning the Île de Nantes (an island in downtown Nantes), this inspired architect uses a method that is sensitive and in the spirit of the place. He advances by subtle, gradual modifications and thereby achieves some "amazingly profound transformations."

Alexandre Chemetoff's Bamboo Garden in the Parc de la Villette, Paris, France.

GILLES CLÉMENT

Who is he?

A key figure on the landscape scene in France, notably since the exhibition he curated at La Villette, *Le jardin planétaire* (The Planetary Garden), Gilles Clément, born in Argenton-sur-Creuse in 1943, is a landscape architect, agronomist, writer, and gardener. He teaches at the École Nationale Supérieure du Paysage in Versailles and recently started giving "lessons" at the Collège de France. Not only does he design parks and gardens, he has also written many theoretical and practical essays. Known for his radical positions and sincere commitment to ecology, Clément puts his theories into practice, both in his projects and exhibitions and in his own garden in the Creuse department in central France.

His work

Gilles Clément has designed a great many gardens and public and private parks. He designed the Jardins de l'Arche in La Défense business district, and worked on Paris's historic East–West axis to the west of La Défense. He is responsible for the Parc Matisse in the Euralille quarter of Lille, with Derborence Island, where he addresses the concept of the wild garden in which no human intervention is allowed, in an inaccessible spot on top of a concrete plateau covering almost 32,000 square feet (3,000 square meters). Among his many other projects, he designed the abbey gardens in Valloires, the garden at the Château de Blois, the Domaine du Rayol gardens, the garden of the Musée des Arts Premiers on Quai Branly, with Jean Nouvel, and the garden of the École Normale Supérieure de Gerland in Lyon. Alongside Allain Provost and Patrick Berger for the greenhouses, Clément was a member of the teams that designed the Parc André-Citroën in Paris.

As early as 1992, he was linked to the Centre Européen Écologique de Terre Vivante project (222 acres/90 hectares); in 1995, at Clermont-Ferrand, he was involved in the Vulcania project, the Centre Européen du Volcanisme (148 acres/60 hectares). He has also completed many other fascinating projects, such as the roof on the submarine base at Saint-Nazaire, the Nettle Garden for the Melle contemporary art biennial, the botanical gardens at Papéari, and so on.

His philosophy

Gilles Clément is the author of the "Planetary Garden" theory, devised on the basis of the finite ecology and the global melting pot. This phenomenon is the outcome of the continual stirring of flows around the planet—winds, ocean currents, animals, and humans on the move, whereby conveyed species are being constantly mixed and redistributed. The underlying philosophy borrows directly from the Garden in Motion idea: "to act as far as possible with, as little as possible against." The end purpose of the Planetary Garden is to figure out how to make use of the diversity in nature without destroying it. Since 1977, Clément has been applying the Garden in Motion theory to his own garden in central France where, instead of restricting plants to a given spot, to organize an artificial creation, he allows his plantings to keep "redrawing" the garden, which now has a shape that will not be the same in the same place when next it flowers. The "third landscape" is another of his areas of concern, and designates "the sum of the spaces in which man leaves landscape evolution to nature alone." It refers to "urban and rural wastelands, transitional spaces, derelict land, swamps, moors, peat bogs, and also roadsides, river banks, railroad embankments, etc." The third landscape is the preferred area for biological diversity to take hold. For Clément it is the planet's genetic reservoir, the space of the future. Taking the third landscape into account as a biological necessity—upon which the future of living creatures depends—changes how we view the territory and sees as valuable spots that usually count for nothing.

The planetary melting pot is a threat to diversity, but leads to novel behavior patterns, new landscapes, and sometimes new species as well. The garden, taken in its traditional sense, is a special place for such planetary mixing. For Clément, the garden today can help us to devise new and respectful, responsible behaviors, and new ways of living in our world.

Derborence Island—an "unreachable" space where nature is left to its own devices—designed by Gilles Clément,
Parc Matisse, Lille, France.

MICHEL CORAJOUD

Who is he?

Born in Annecy, in southeastern France, on July 14, 1937, Michel Corajoud has a dual background. A graduate of the national art and design college, the École Nationale Supérieure des Arts Décoratifs, he also holds a diploma in landscape architecture from the Ministry of Agriculture. He first worked with the landscape architect Jacques Simon from 1964 to 1966. Then, from 1966 to 1975, he worked with Henri Ciriani and Borja Huidobro, in association with the Atelier d'Urbanisme et d'Architecture. Since 1975 Corajoud has been in partnership with his wife Claire Corajoud, a graduate of the national horticultural college, the École Nationale Supérieure d'Horticulture. Seen as one of the founders of the revival of the landscape architect's profession in France, Michel Corajoud was the first to take issue with his predecessors' basically nature-related view, whereby "knowledge about the city and architecture was ignored." For him, the landscape should be "an introductory form of architecture, due to the continuity of intent required between buildings and the outdoor spaces that they determine."

A teacher at the École Nationale Supérieure du Paysage in Versailles, he was one of the key players in transforming this school of landscape architecture. He was also visiting professor at the University of Geneva's Institute of Architecture(1999–2002). In December 2003, Michel Corajoud was awarded the Grand Prix de l'Urbanisme, a prize for urban planning in France.

His work

Michel Corajoud's oeuvre is impressive. He has designed many parks: the Parc Jean-Verlhac (or Parc de la Villeneuve) in Grenoble and the Parc des Coudrays in Élancourt-Maurepas in 1974; the Parc du Sausset in the Seine-Saint-Denis department near Paris in 1981; the Parc Paysager at Les Jardins d'Éole in Paris with Claire Corajoud in 2004; the Parc de Gerland in Lyon, with Claire Corajoud, between 1999 and 2006; and redeveloped the site at the old Falck steelworks in Sesto San Giovanni with Renzo Piano in 2006.

He has also designed numerous developments in public spaces: Quai and Boulevard Charles-de-Gaulle in Lyon with Renzo Piano in 1996; Avenue d'Italie in Paris with Pierre Gangnet and the covering of the A1 turnpike in 1998; Boulevard Tony-Garnier in Lyon, with Pierre Gangnet, in 1998–2006; the left bank quaysides in Bordeaux with Claire Corajoud between 2000 and 2008; the areas upstream and downstream from the Cité Internationale in Lyon with Renzo Piano in 2001; the Place Antonin-Perrin in Lyon and the Quais de Loire in Orléans with Pierre Gangnet in 2005–6.

His philosophy

Michel Corajoud is among the leading landscape players in France. He is also an outstanding theoretician. Working most of the time on large-scale projects, he is always careful—before doing anything—to pay great attention to the existing natural and architectural elements. He also attaches great importance to how plant species develop. He is careful most of all to "propose spaces that offer a pretext for the imagination." As he explains, "The landscape is where the sky and the earth touch. . . . To look at the countryside is to experience and make one's own the meaning of the labor that brought it about, it is to capture in one's own body the dynamics of realization, it is to rediscover the dividing lines, the thresholds, the successive coverings. It is to gain a hazy understanding of the history of the succeeding generations that set up this drapery, albeit without being able to overcome the site's points of resistance, like that rock that keeps bursting through the surface."

The redevelopment of the quayside in Bordeaux is an outstanding success, and its most spectacular feature is the extraordinary Water Mirror, set facing the Place de la Bourse.

Green hills in the Parc des Coudrays designed by Michel Corajoud, Élancourt, Yvelines, France.

PASCAL CRIBIER

VVho is he?

Born in Normandy in 1953, the French landscape architect Pascal Cribier left school at the age of fourteen, preferring to join the French go-carting team. Later he studied at the extremely open university of Vincennes (Université de Paris VIII) before joining the visual arts department at the national fine arts college, the École Nationale Supérieure des Beaux-Arts, moving towards architecture, and gaining a diploma in architecture in 1978. Influenced by a two-year spell at a nursery, he decided to become a landscape architect. Directed by Laurent Le Bon, the exhibition he mounted in 2008, *Les Racines ont des feuilles* (Roots Have Leaves), and the book describing his work both provide the keys to interpreting his original output, which is attentive to its surroundings both visible and invisible.

His vvork

Pascal Cribier has completed numerous projects. After a landscape and architectural survey of the Pays de Caux region of northern France, he undertook over seventy projects, among which were, in 1982, the lagooning of waste water in the village of Ermenouville, and the development of a logging park in Limésy, followed by, in 1989, creation of the Donjon de Vez gardens in the Oise region. Most of these projects were designed with the landscape architect and urban planner Patrick Écoutin, with whom, from 1995 to 2005, he conducted urban surveys with a view to redeveloping industrial areas in greater Lyon. Since 2006, he has been working on the former Lille Fives factories with Djamel Klouche. He designed the patio for the Bastille Opera House and the IRCAM gardens in Paris. The Tuileries Gardens works, begun in 1990 with Louis Benech and François Roubaud, show off his approach in a public garden.

Alongside Philippe Starck, he reconfigured the art and design college, the École Nationale Supérieure des Arts Décoratifs. With the botanist Patrick Blanc he created the amazing Experimental Garden of Méry-sur-Oise. In 1994, in Aramon, in Provence, he designed the garden, Le Plaisir, for Jacques Hollander, around a house improved by the architect Jean-Michel Wilmotte.

He designed the grounds and garden at Woolton House in Hampshire, United Kingdom, in 1995. In 1999, he redesigned the 86,490 acres (35,000 hectares) of the La Cense stud farm in Dillon, Montana. He transformed Motu Tane Island off Bora Bora with some spectacular new plantings.

And, of course, he devotes a great deal of effort to his "laboratory garden" on the Normandy coast, which is where this very busy landscape architect recharges his batteries.

His philosophy

For Pascal Cribier, "creating a garden is first of all meeting a backer and a site.... The gardens we create are totally artificial." His favorite mantra is "Nothing is less comfortable than nature, no one can live there, it is often by no means hospitable." As for landscapes, it is human activities—in the quest for high performance and efficiency—that shape them. Although he has great respect for the trees and plants he selects for his projects, Cribier knows that "the art of the landscape designer is to constrain that nature." He is careful over every detail, every structure, every arrangement, understanding their importance in the overall garden. He knows too that you have to allow for plants having different life cycles. "Trees, shrubs and perennials all grow at different speeds, they do not have the same life 'expectancy.'... I arrange for these 'garden times' to become superimposed, in harmony. That part of my work I find fascinating. And when a particular atmosphere takes hold of a few friends meeting together in the garden, and they enjoy the moment, you are touching on the essence of the garden," declares this landscape architect, convinced that "each and every place can become the most beautiful spot in the world."

TOP: *Garden of Pleasure, Aramon, France.* CENTER: *Woolton House gardens, Woolton Hill, United Kingdom.*

BOTTOM: *Experimental Garden, Méry-sur-Oise, France.*

IAN HAMILTON FINLAY

Who is he?

Ian Hamilton Finlay (1925–2006) was born in the Bahamas and was sent at the age of six to boarding school in Scotland, a country where he spent the rest of his life. As a teenager, he already knew he would become an artist, as we see from his paintings, engravings, plays, and poems from that period. An artist with a passion for history and philosophy, he put a great deal of his energy into creating and developing his garden, Little Sparta, although many of his works are on display or held in the collections of major European museums. An artist, writer, poet, sculptor, and garden designer, Ian Hamilton Finlay is the author of a multifaceted and sometimes controversial oeuvre.

His work

In 1964, Ian Hamilton Finlay founded a publishing house, the Wild Hawthorn Press, as an introduction to his subsequent sculptural work. In 1966, he moved with his wife to a remote part of the Scottish moors, to the abandoned farm in Stonypath, where he designed his famous garden, Little Sparta. He decorated this with temples, sculptures, ruins, porticoes; it became a place of creativity and of poetic, philosophical, and even political provocation. Drawing inspiration from ancient Greece and Rome, the heroes of the French Revolution and the last wars, his garden echoes the upheavals that have swept through our Western societies.

With its water features, its clearings, its stone benches, its graves, its obelisks, and its bridges over waterfalls and streams, this constantly changing garden, exploring the conflicting relationship between culture and nature, is both art and poetry, playing with words as well as with forms.

His philosophy

A conceptual artist, and a writer as well, Ian Hamilton Finlay comes across as an atypical personality who used the garden as a means of expressing his world view and his poetical, artistic, and political ideas. A committed artist, battling on several fronts, using the reference to antiquity in order to fight against the absurdity of modern utilitarian liberalism, he was also fascinated by the French Revolution. In all Hamilton Finlay's works, and most notably in his garden, Little Sparta, we find words, inscriptions, and sentences either invented by the artist or famous quotations, scattered around the gloomy Scottish moor, as marks of his commitment to the international movement of "concrete poetry," of which he was an influential member. For all its singularity, his philosophical garden possesses an indefinable and powerful charm.

Ponds and buildings of the Temple Pool Garden in the Little Sparta Garden, Dunsyre, United Kingdom.

ÉDOUARD FRANÇOIS

VVho is he?

Édouard François, born in Paris in 1958, is an alumnus of the fine arts college, the École Nationale des Beaux-Arts, a graduate of École des Ponts et Chaussées engineering school, and an architect and urban planner since 1986. He partnered
François Roche from 1990 until 1993, and Duncan Lewis from 1994 until 1997, before finally setting up his own architectural, urban planning, and design agency in 1998.

His work very quickly came to the attention of critics and he has taught at some of the most prestigious French architectural, garden, and landscape schools—including the École Méditerranéenne des Jardins et du Paysage in Grasse, the École
Spéciale d'Architecture in Paris, and the École Nationale Supérieure du Paysage in Versailles—and abroad, notably at the
renowned Architectural Association in London. François is a member of the Architectes Français à l'Export Association and
of the general committee of the Institut Français d'Architecture.

The admission of his works into the permanent collections of the Centre Pompidou and of the FRAC contemporary art
center is evidence of genuine plaudits from the architectural community. François' work has been regularly shown abroad,
notably at the Canadian Center for Architecture in Montreal, at the Épreuve d'Artiste Gallery in Beirut, at the Guggenheim
Museum in New York City, at the Architecture Gallery in Leipzig, and at the Victoria 8 Albert Museum in London.

His vvork

VVhile Édouard François was spotted very early on for his works standing midway between architecture
and landscape—he was noticed for his soft greenhouses presented at the 1996 Chaumont-sur-Loire
International Garden Festival, for example—he is especially well known for his pro-environmental commitment, notably with the Building That Grows (2000) in Montpellier (seven floors with automatically irrigated
plants on the facade), the Flower Tower (2001), and the Bamboo Building in Paris, the eighteen organic brick
and chestnut housing units that he designed in Louviers. He also made a name for himself with his interior
design operations in Clichy, his Paris showrooms, and for the Havas Group in Suresnes, not forgetting his "tree
school" in Thiais (1996). It is with his sophisticated concepts for building in historic town centers, the moulé-
troué (cast and punctured) and the muré-troué (walled and punctured) methods, that François confirmed
his reputation in the world of contemporary creation with the Hôtel Fouquet's Barrière on the Champs-
Élysées in Paris, and the BMVV Showroom on the Boulevard de VVaterloo in Brussels. In charge of the major
conversion works on the Samaritaine department store in Paris, which he covered with indoor and outdoor
gardens, he has also built two green towers, the M6B2 in Paris and one in Nantes.

His philosophy

Viewed as the pioneer of "green architecture," as an environmentalist pioneer with his amazing buildings
with frontages of plants (such as Flower Tower, SkinVVall, Eden Bio), Édouard François is an atypical personality within the architectural community, with his subtle combination of rigor, pragmatism, and unbridled
creativity. An enemy of compartmentalization, inquisitive about everything, François is interested in every
domain, stimulated by the diversity of problems and issues, passing seamlessly from luxury to social housing and undeterred by any contemporary architectural problem. For example, he is conducting an in-depth
inquiry into the issue of parking lots. He adjusts to the context and to the human element to devise unique,
accessible projects, and can boast of having touched on every style, "from the school building to social housing, and from luxury hotels to sewage treatment plants."

The experiments in connection with preserving biodiversity that he is conducting in Paris and Nantes show
just how important his thinking on green architecture is to his work. Even though he thinks architecture
"needs to know when to make itself scarce" and blend in with the surroundings, Édouard François is searching for the perfect aesthetic as much as he is for compliance with sustainable development. He is not done
yet with "growing walls" and deploying his gardens about town.

Project for the Alliance Française in New Delhi, India.

KATHRYN GUSTAFSON

Who is she?

Kathryn Gustafson, an American landscape architect born in Washington State in 1951, started studying fashion design at the Fashion Institute of Technology in New York City. A stylist in New York and Paris during the 1970s, while working with textiles she began to be fascinated with the fluidity of lines and forms. Much taken with the works of Jacques Sgard, she studied landscape architecture at the landscape architecture college, the École Nationale Supérieure du Paysage in Versailles, graduating in 1979. As a landscape architect working on public commissions, she very soon won a series of major landscaping project competitions in France. Being in great demand, Gustafson is currently working worldwide from her two offices, Gustafson Porter in London, and Gustafson Guthrie Nichol in Seattle.

Her work

Among her many achievements, some projects helped more than others to build up her reputation, like the gardens at the corporate headquarters for Shell, Esso, and L'Oréal near Paris, the Jardins de l'Imaginaire in Terrasson, the Place des Droits-de-l'Homme in Évry, and the Square Rachmaninov in Paris. Other major works include the Diana Princess of Wales Memorial Fountain in London's Hyde Park, the Arthur Ross Terrace at the American Museum of Natural History in New York, and the new Millennium Park in Chicago. She has won many prizes, including the Chrysler Design Award.

Her philosophy

Kathryn Gustafson is known for her "openly artistic stance." With each new project, searching for the genius loci, she plays upon abstraction, clarity, and simple images. The deliberately limited number of materials she uses (stone, trees, and shrubs) lends power and consistency to her work. Terraces, slopes, ponds, and fountains often feature as markers of her fluid, poetical style, mixing fragments of history with tradition and a contemporary view of the landscape. Gentle cascades and winding pathways of water, refined objects in suspension, like the golden ribbon set around the trees in Terrasson, planted tunnels, and sacred groves all bear the stamp of her unusual sensitivity, grace, and delicacy.

The undulating land in the landscaped areas of Morbras and Shell Petroleum in Rueil-Malmaison, the shaping of the landscape at the entrance to the Marseilles superhighway, the skillful and poetic layering of the Jardins de l'Imaginaire in Terrasson are examples of her instantly recognizable style. Gustafson is fond of playing with the line of the horizon, confronting often geometric forms and different scales, to delight visitors by imperceptibly disturbing their visual perceptions.

Terraces of the Gardens of the Imagination, Terrasson, France.

RICHARD HAAG

Who is he?

The son of a nurseryman, who taught him the importance of the landscape and ecology at an early age, the American landscape architect Richard Haag, born in Kentucky in 1923, studied architecture and landscape architecture at the University of Illinois, then at the University of California, Berkeley. In 1952, he obtained a master's degree in landscape architecture from the renowned Harvard Graduate School of Design. In 1954 and 1955, he spent two years on a Fulbright grant in Kyoto, which was to influence his later work. Back in the United States, he worked from 1956 to 1957 for Lawrence Halprin in San Francisco, then set up his own agency in the Bay area. He went on to found the landscape architecture department at the University of Washington's College of Architecture and Urban Planning. Richard Haag is a researcher with the American Society of Landscape Architects (ASLA), honorary member of the American Institute of Architects, and a former resident at the American Academy in Rome. He is the only landscape architect to have won the ASLA medal twice.

His work

Having designed over five hundred projects, Richard Haag is best known for two major works, the Gas Works Park Lake Union in Seattle (1971–88) and the Bloedel Reserve (1979–84) on Bainbridge Island in Puget Sound. For the former project, going counter to all the other submissions, and ahead of the regeneration experiments on disused industrial plants, he decided to preserve the refinery infrastructure and include it in the park design, rather than to eliminate it altogether. He then found solutions in terms of detoxifying the soil contaminated with hydrocarbons through an original bioremediation method, by adding organic material to encourage the growth of soil microorganisms.

At the Bloedel Reserve, located in a forest near Seattle, Haag created a series of landscapes and garden rooms, the best known being the Reflection Garden, which is bordered with clipped yews, in a perfectly rectangular clearing, amid some magnificent Douglas firs and with a water mirror reflecting the trees and sky. The park also has a very fine Moss Garden. Haag has completed many other works in Seattle, Berkeley, Washington, and elsewhere.

His philosophy

Possessing an encyclopedic knowledge of plants and horticulture, Richard Haag always speaks about long-term strategies for the development of the parks and gardens he designs. He advocates direct contact with sites and attaches the utmost importance to intuition. Influenced by both his country roots and his Japanese experience of Zen gardens, he has a stated preference for simple forms. His work is renowned for its creativeness, its sensitivity to the natural environment, and the use of existing structures and reliefs.

A water mirror in the Reflection Garden, Bloedel Reserve, near Seattle, United States.

CHARLES JENCKS

Who is he?

Born in Baltimore on June 21, 1939, Charles Jencks is an American landscape architect and designer based in Scotland, and is renowned worldwide for his theories on postmodern architecture. He studied English literature at Harvard, obtained a master's degree in architecture from Harvard's Graduate School of Design, and later a doctoral degree in architecture from London University's Bartlett School of Architecture.

He has been a lecturer or visiting lecturer at over forty universities worldwide, notably in Beijing, Shanghai, Tokyo, Milan, and Barcelona, and in the United States at Harvard, Columbia, Princeton, and Yale, with numerous publications to his name. As a universally respected architect and essayist, he applied his theories to the 30 acres (12 hectares) of his Portrack House property near Dumfries, Scotland. His outstanding Garden of Cosmic Speculation, which he began with his wife Maggie Keswick in 1989, is probably one of the most spectacular contemporary gardens.

His work

In Edinburgh, together with Terry Farrell and Duncan Whatmore, Charles Jencks designed a remarkable landscaped relief in front of the Scottish National Gallery of Modern Art. He has also designed symbolic furniture, from the Garagia Rotunda in Cape Cod, produced in 1976–77, the Elemental House in Los Angeles, and the Thematic House in London, with Terry Farrell. He also created the Center for Life in Newcastle, which was opened in May of 2000. He is working in Northumberland on a massive "green goddess" project, a giant plant sculpture of a woman reclining on the ground, made up of 1.65 tons (1.5 million metric tons) of coal-mining waste.

His philosophy

Charles Jencks's work is deeply influenced by science and philosophy. He believes that contemporary science is the greatest moving force in our time. His creative landscapes are a meditation on man's place in the universe, the garden being for him the ideal spot for meditating and speculating on our relation to the cosmos. His work is inspired by biology, genetics, chaos theory, and much of the basic research done in physics and medicine.

Giant checkerboards, blood-red bridges, gently undulating hills delicately grassed in utopian shapes, time spirals, water mirrors, galactic benches, mazes, fractals, diagrams, circular paths corresponding to the wanderings of the mind, double spiral stairs, and sculptures in the image of the double helix of DNA are some of the strange figures and structures that populate the fantastic world of the Garden of Cosmic Speculation. With its fascinatingly unusual hill shapes, like the Snake Mound or the Snail Mound, with gentle slopes that you climb slowly, rising skywards, this perfectly harmonious landscape has a profound effect on the visitor's soul. It is a spot where you feel at peace, in tune with the world and with yourself.

Just like Chinese gardens, of which his wife was an eminent specialist, Charles Jencks's garden is a microcosm of the universe, depicting the contemporary world's cosmic and cultural evolution. With each creature striving to increase its knowledge, understand what is going on, what is going to happen, and how things evolve, this cosmic passion marks both the desire to know and the dream of connectedness with the universe. For Jencks, gardens are like autobiographies: they reveal the happy moments, the tragedies, and the truths of a being. This is an exceptionally powerful and profound work that he has been inscribing, year after year, in the harsh Scottish countryside.

Spiral hills in the Garden of Cosmic Speculation, at Portrack House, near Dumfries, United Kingdom.

DAN URBAN KILEY

Who is he?

Born in Boston in 1912, the American landscape architect Daniel Urban Kiley, who died in 2004, was heavily influenced by his childhood vacations on his grandmother's New Hampshire ranch. He served a four-year apprenticeship with the landscape designer Warren H. Manning, before attending Harvard University in 1936 to study landscape architecture, at the very moment when Walter Gropius and his Bauhaus followers came on the scene. Kiley left Harvard in 1938 without graduating. He worked for a short time for the National Park Service in Concord, New Hampshire, then at the United States Housing Authority, which he left on the advice of the architect Louis Kahn to open his own office, initially operating in New Hampshire and later in Vermont.

From 1943 to 1945, Kiley served in the US Army. At the end of World War II, after designing the courtroom for the Nuremberg trials, he visited the major European gardens, most notably the parks designed by André Le Nôtre at Sceaux, Chantilly, Versailles, and Vaux-le-Vicomte, and their geometric character was to have a great influence upon his later classical modernist style.

Unlike many of his contemporaries, Daniel Urban Kiley was a pure practitioner who neither published any books, nor taught at university, and he never joined the American Society of Landscape Architects.

His work

In 1947, Daniel Urban Kiley won the Jefferson National Expansion Memorial competition along with Eero Saarinen. In 1955, again with Saarinen, he designed the Miller Garden in Columbus, Indiana, often viewed as the most important postwar garden in the United States. In 1963, he designed the gardens at Washington airport, based on an idea of Saarinen's.

In 1968, with Walter Kiley Netch, he designed the gardens for the new Air Force Academy in Colorado Springs, Colorado; then, in 1969, some remarkable garden terraces in Oakland, California, followed by dozens of public and private projects, such as the Dallas Museum of Art Sculpture Garden in 1983, and, in 1985, the gardens for Fountain Place in Dallas, Texas. For this building by architects Pei and Cobb, which stands opposite the Bank of America Plaza, he designed a water garden with four hundred fountains. A refreshing spot to meet people in the city, planted with bald cypresses in round granite plant boxes, and surrounded by terrace pools with cascades on several levels, this place has a highly poetic design.

In 1988, Kiley designed the Nations Bank Plaza complex in Tampa, Florida, with Harry Wolf, and the elegant Henry Moore Sculpture Garden of the Nelson Atkins Art Museum in Kansas City, Missouri. This patriarch of architecture and landscape designed over nine hundred projects and won countless awards.

His philosophy

Kiley's works display both the clarity of the French garden—if we examine the geometric layout of the paths, trees, water, and lawns—and an inspiration drawn directly from contemporary architecture. His use of hedges and walls, for instance, is clearly influenced by the work of Ludwig Mies van der Rohe. In his gardens, geometry is fundamental. Rather than copying and trying to imitate the curvilinear shapes of nature, he asserted a mathematical order for the landscape. Whatever the circumstances, according to him works should be "appropriate" to their natural or urban surroundings. Kiley also attached great importance to the choice of available plants, which sometimes even preceded his design of a garden.

Miller House gardens, Columbus, United States.

BERNARD LASSUS

Who is he?

Born in Chamalières, France, in 1929, Bernard Lassus enrolled at the École Nationale Supérieure des Beaux-Arts (ENSBA) in Paris and was then a regular visitor to the Louvre and the Musée Guimet. He initially embarked on an artist's career, with a passion for color and light, joining the ENSBA teaching staff in 1968. What led him to landscaping was a study on color in the villages and landscapes of Corsica. He began to teach during the 1960s, in a department of the École Nationale Supérieure d'Horticulture in Versailles, and at the École Nationale Supérieure d'Architecture in La Villette. In 1972, he set up the research center the Centre National d'Étude et de Recherche du Paysage for the Fondation de l'École Nationale Supérieure du Paysage in Versailles, where he headed the Charles-Rivière-Dufresny workshop. Enjoying a considerable international reputation, and the author of many theoretical works, he was rewarded for his landscape work with the Grand Prix du Paysage in 1996. He received the Sir Geoffrey Jellicoe gold medal from the International Federation of Landscape Architects—UNESCO in 2009. He received honorary degrees from the Université de Montréal in 2002, from Leibniz Universität Hannover in 2006, and from the Università IUAV di Venezia in 2007. He won the science medal from the University of Bologna's Istituto di Studi Avanzati in 2010. He teaches at the University of Pennsylvania.

His work

Bernard Lassus has written numerous important studies on landscape. He has completed major commissions from the French state for turnpike rest areas. He designed the Jardin des Retours in Rochefort, Charente-Maritime for which he received the Grand Prix du Patrimoine heritage award from the Ministry of Culture. He designed the Black Garden in Boulogne-Billancourt for the Renault automobile manufacturer in 1967, the coloring of the La Maurelette buildings in Marseille (1962–67), housing in Quétigny-les-Dijon, and green facades at Évry (1971–78). He has also designed rest areas on many French highways (Angers-Tours, Alençon-le Mans), the Garden of Optical Bushes in Niort (1993), and the Hanging Gardens of Colas in Paris (2000–7).

His philosophy

Taking the view that the gap between gardens and landscapes is getting smaller, that "garden" and "landscape" are "in the process of becoming intertwined, when they used to be so different and sometimes opposites," Bernard Lassus is convinced that the garden is landscape. In fact, he often prefers the notion of "ambience" to that of landscape—touch, smell, and sound being for him senses that are now often added to the sight of the landscape.

A remarkable theoretician, often taking different paths to his peers—he coined the term *habitants-paysagistes* (landscaper-inhabitants)—he is convinced that we are all creators who are more or less aware of the landscape. He was also one of the first landscape architects willing to accept the space of the expressway as a landscape. For him, new landscapes are being deployed in ways that have changed our perceptions and brought a new dimension to the land. The expressway is to a certain degree a "belvedere," but a "mobile belvedere," from which the objects perceived dance in a ballet of contradictory movements. The rest areas, he says, are intermediate places, like gardens of landscapes, "picked spots," an introduction to the country. According to him, the landscape is not "movement," it is transformation. The art of gardens and the art of landscaping are arts of transformation and not of copycat repetition.

He is always keen to mix in the natural and the artificial, which he frequently uses for his work on color, such as the roof gardens of Colas, designed with perforated sheets carved into the shape of trees or shrubs, and painted in various colors to represent the four seasons.

The Optical Bushes—chromatic experiments in Niort, France.

PETER LATZ

Who is he?

Born in Darmstadt in 1939, the German landscape architect Peter Latz, who teaches land-scape architecture and studied in Munich and at Aachen University, founded his Latz and Partner agency in Saarbrücken, in 1968, with his wife Anneliese. He joined the teaching staff at the Gesamthochschule in Kassel in 1973, before taking up a post as landscape architecture professor at the Technische Universität of München in Munich, from 1983 to 2008. Now retired, he is associate professor at the University of Pennsylvania in Philadelphia and is also visiting professor at the Harvard Graduate School of Design. He was awarded the First Rosa Barba European Landscape Prize in Barcelona for his design of the Landschaftspark Duisburg-Nord in 2000, the Grand Prix d'Urbanisme de l'Académie d'Architecture in Paris in 2001, the EDRA/*Places* award for design at Edmond, United States, in 2005, and the Green Good Design Prize in 2009.

His work

Peter Latz has risen to international prominence by developing, from 1991 to 2001, the Landschaftspark Duisburg-Nord landscape park, designed on the 570-acre (230-hectare) site of a disused steelworks in the Ruhr. This spot is a benchmark for reclamation of disused industrial sites and is characterized by the designer's wish not to conceal its industrial past but, on the contrary, to make it the central feature of the park, which is designed around the ruins of the steel mill. Latz began by detoxifying the soil contaminated by industrial waste, then cleaning up the River Emscher, and reusing materials that allowed rainwater collection. Then he transformed the landfill into walks, the gas holders into pools, and the rusty indus-trial buildings into metal cathedrals, giving them a new lease of life by creating clipped hedges, bosks, and rose gardens all around them. He was also behind development work at the uni-versity and university hospital in Marburg (1976–80), the port of Saarbrücken (1979–89), Granta Park in Cambridge, United Kingdom (1997), the Science City in Ulm (1988–2001), the Green Belt in Frankfurt (1990–92), the Plateau de Kirchberg in Luxembourg (1990–2008), the Parco Dora in Turin since 2004, and the Ariel Sharon Park in Tel Aviv since 2004.

His philosophy

Peter Latz is passionate about environmental issues, and whatever he does elaborates on his theory of site reclamation. Whether it be the Emscher Park steel mill in Duisburg, or the Hiriya Landfill Restoration in Israel, with its 1,977 acres (800 hectares) of contaminated soil turned into ecological parks, he is constantly regenerating places destroyed by human activ-ity and turning them into a kind of paradise.

He shows a special affinity for this type of site. "I grew up in an industrial area, in Saarland," he explains. He is fully familiar with the "ambiguity" of such places: "For the people who live there, they are the best places in the world. And when they close down, they get mad." His method is to leave enough elements for people to recognize what used to be there, but to turn these places into gardens or oases.

Orchards in blossom in the shade of the steel mill, Emscher Park, Duisburg, Germany.

ISAMU NOGUCHI

Who is he?

Born in Los Angeles to a Scottish mother and a Japanese father, the Japanese designer Isamu Noguchi (1904–1988) spent his childhood years in Japan and initially studied medicine before opting for a more artistic career.

Keen to draw inspiration from the sources of his Eastern culture, and wanting to reclaim the special relationship with nature that he had enjoyed in childhood, he went to Kyoto in 1931 to study traditional pottery, clay, and drawing techniques. In the United States, having a passion for the world of dancing, he worked with the choreographer Martha Graham. This multifaceted artist established links with the New York and international art community and made a name for himself in the 1940s. Back in Japan in the early 1950s, the artist devoted himself to the art of the garden.

His work

A sculptor, decorator, designer, and creator of gardens, Noguchi was a complete artist. The gardens he produced at Keio University and at the Metropolitan Museum of Art in New York are artworks in their own right, engaging in a richly meaningful dialogue with the architecture. In 1956, he produced some large stone sculptures for the UNESCO gardens in Paris. This garden combines the traditional Japanese spirit with Noguchi's very contemporary artistic vision. He also designed a number of gardens (Billy Rose Art Garden at the Israel Museum in Jerusalem, the Kodomo no Kuni children's garden in Tokyo). Well known for his lamps, which are veritable light sculptures, he also designed some magnificent fountains, like the one at Expo 70 in Osaka.

His philosophy

Isamu Noguchi's dual culture, his extremely varied education, and his numerous trips from East to West made him an outstandingly creative personality, open to many different art forms. With respect to gardens, Noguchi introduced a new form, successfully designing a perfectly controlled natural environment in line with the visual research behind his sculpture.

Avoiding any copying of tradition, bending the codes, he devised novel forms, linking man, architecture, and nature in new ways. Thus his UNESCO garden is presented in its entirety to the visitor, displaying clear lines, thereby breaking the rules of the traditional garden. Also, contrary to the customary codes, he had no compunction in introducing contemporary materials into the plant world, for the wealth of his imagination led him to innovate in this area, just as it did in his sculpture.

UNESCO garden, Paris, France.

PIET OUDOLF

Who is he?

Dutchman Piet Oudolf was born on October 27, 1944; since 1982 he has been living not far from Arnhem, near Hummelo, right on the German border. A matchless nursery gardener with an extensive knowledge of plants, a remarkable hybridizer of perennials, an ecologist and adept of the natural garden, he has only been designing gardens in the last few years, with huge success. It should be mentioned that this outstanding colorist is viewed as being one of the key players in the new wave of landscape architecture.

His work

Apart from creating his wonderful private garden, Piet Oudolf also designed the beds at the De Uithof botanical gardens at Universiteit Utrecht, the approaches to the ABN AMRO Bank in Amsterdam, the Dream Park in Enköping near Stockholm in Sweden, and the Staudenmaschsee Park in Hanover, Germany.

In Britain, he designed the entrance to the Pensthorpe Waterfowl Trust in Fakenham, Norfolk, and some large private gardens in Bentley, Hampshire and for Jesus College in Cambridge. He had a hand in one of the courtyards of Hampton Court Palace, and designed two huge "borders" for the Royal Horticultural Society in Wisley, Surrey, as well as a wall-lined garden at Scampston in 2004.

In the United States, Oudolf was chosen to design the Gardens of Remembrance in New York City, a place for meditation close to the site of the World Trade Center Twin Towers, destroyed on September 11, 2001. With Kathryn Gustafson he designed Millennium Park in Chicago. He is also responsible for the conversion of the amazing New York High Line and Battery Park.

His philosophy

His in-depth knowledge of plants, their growth, and their development from season to season, enables Piet Oudolf to play like a painter with plant structures and textures, just as well as with their colors.

He works in great sheets of bright colors, vibrant with light. He is interested in both the inflorescences and the stems and foliage of the plants he chooses, with a predilection for the outline and supple elegance of grasses, which is what first earned him his reputation. The feelings stirred by his gardens come from the constant quivering of tall grasses, pale, watered, soft, thin, or transparent, depending on the time of day.

The effect of the seasons and the weather on plants, things like wind, rain, dew, ice, frost, and snow, as well as the presence of garden fauna such as cobwebs, plays a major role in his plant selection. The plants are full participants in the garden design.

Another concern of his is minimum maintenance and an environmentally friendly approach, cultivating a felicitous combination of "the wild and the controlled." "For me," says Oudolf, "plants are never tall enough. But I don't scatter giants all over the place just any old how. In large spaces, the main purpose they serve is as an anchor point for the eye."

"The view that I have developed, and especially in my work on perennials, is based not only on respect for nature, but also on the power, the energy, the emotions, the beauty, and aesthetics that nature produces," he explains.

Waves of Piet Oudolf's pink grasses, Millennium Park, Pensthorpe, United Kingdom.

RUSSELL PAGE

VVho is he?

Top British botanist, a landscape architect in great demand both in Europe and in the United States, and an indefatigable traveler, Russell Page (1906–1985) was doubtless one of the greatest garden designers of the late twentieth century.

He studied at the Slade School of Fine Art in London, and later in Paris, where his intense passion for plants led him to embark upon a career as a professional landscape architect.

His vvork

In Italy he designed some very large private gardens, like the Villa Landriana gardens in Torre San Lorenzo near Rome, comprising thirty extraordinary garden rooms, the La Mortella Gardens in Ischia, a secret garden nestling at the bottom of a very shady valley, which receives in its amazingly tropical atmosphere many of the intellectual and artistic elite of Europe, and the San Liberato Gardens in Bracciano, laden with roses. He also created, in the United States, the US National Arboretum Garden in Washington, and in Britain Badminton Park, in Badminton, Somerset, as well as the extraordinary garden of the Cheddar Gorge restaurant. He was also responsible for the restoration work on the Port Lympne Gardens in Kent and the garden at the Frick Collection in New York.

His clients included the Duke and Duchess of Windsor, King Leopold of Belgium, the Agnelli family, the Rothschilds, Babe and William S. Paley, and Marcel Boussac. Becoming personally involved in making each garden, he was known for his great modesty and total unselfishness.

His philosophy

A perfect connoisseur of every garden style, Russell Page designed landscape works that were both geometric and poetic, adapting with great flexibility to every universe, every culture and every climate. Thoroughly understanding his clients' requirements, Page knew how to capture the genius loci, adjust perfectly to the plant environment, modify spaces, forms and volumes, move hills and streams, create lakes and new paths. The garden rooms at the Villa Landriana, and the amazingly tropical vegetation of La Mortella, as well as his American output, bear the hallmark of a wonderful gardener's imagination and remarkable sensitivity, such was his fondness for mixing rare varieties and achieving novel harmonies of color. But he could also use very few different plant species and bring them together in large beds, thereby producing a unified overall effect. Page would proceed by strictly planned plantings. The intelligence and clarity of the composition were evident in his absolute mastery of green architecture, and his unerring use of yew or box hedges, often framing large patches of flat monochromes.

His final work, in the United States, a large park housing a collection of PepsiCo sculptures surrounded by sublime plantations, is a superbly elegant work of poetry and gardening intelligence.

"I know that I cannot make anything new. To make a garden is to organize all the elements present and add fresh ones, but first of all, I must absorb as best I can all that I see, the sky and the skyline, the soil, the color of the grass and the shape and nature of the trees. Each half-mile of countryside has its own nature and every few yards is a reinterpretation. Each stone where it lies says something of the earth's underlying structure; and the plants growing there, whether native or exotic, will indicate the vegetable chemistry of that one place." Russell Page, *The Education of a Gardener*.

Santolinas and clipped box in the gardens of the Villa Silvio Pelico, Moncalieri, near Turin, Italy.

RENÉ PECHÈRE

Who is he?

René Pechère (1908–2002), a landscape architect born in Ixelles, Belgium, was one of Europe's leading figures in landscapes and gardens. He discovered his calling almost by chance, with Buyssens, the Brussels master of landscape architecture, and attended horticultural college in Vilvorde. He designed upwards of nine hundred private and public gardens in Belgium, France, Germany, and the Netherlands.

As early as 1935, he was involved in designing gardens for the Universal Exhibition in Brussels. In 1952, he became an adviser to the Belgian Ministry of Transport. As a freelance landscape architect, Pechère designed the exterior gardens for the Universal Exhibition of 1958. For that occasion he designed the Congo and Four Seasons gardens, which earned him his international reputation. He also restored many parks, including the château gardens of Beloeil and Seneffe.

This landscape architect, greatly admired by both his peers and his successors, who put his name to nearly a thousand gardens, and who brought to them his highly demanding artistic sense, contrived to find his own aesthetic language for his projects without turning his back on classicism and tradition.

His work

Pechère produced a vast amount of work in Brussels: the exterior amenities at the site of the Belgian French- and Flemish-language radio and television broadcasting companies, Tomberg Park in Woluwe, Ter Coigne Park in Watermael-Boitsfort, and the development of the access ramps to Brussels Zaventem Airport.

Pechère took part in many projects in Brussels during the 1960s and 1970s. To him we owe the Parc Botanique and the Mont-des-Arts garden, the gardens at the Van Buuren Museum, the Berlaymont, and Erasmus House. His achievements are many, including the planting of trees over an underground car park on a minimal layer of soil at the Cité Administrative de l'État in Brussels.

His philosophy

For René Pechère, "the garden and landscape architect is becoming increasingly important, since he makes an essential contribution to the joy of living. He develops spaces as an aesthete and practitioner by bringing amenity to the environment through nature."

In his book *Grammaire des jardins* (A Grammar of Gardens), published in 1987, he explained, "To invent a garden is to modify behavior patterns, habits, and tastes; it is to invent the change of scenery that is appropriate for harmony at once vegetable, animal, and humanist. It is to invent a peace." To his way of thinking, gardens render the philosophical views of the societies that order them. The art of the garden must be "a language animated by the constant desire for the advancement of humanity."

His style, although charming and poetic, is rigorous almost to the point of austerity—and geometric. Pechère used box and yew, or other plants, as architectural features, and attached great importance to rhythms, combinations of colors, and the play of light and shadow. "Plants are words to be arranged into something like a beautiful sentence. The paths and levels are rhythms to a beat." All his gardens show this will to update the classical rules of composition.

While he was fond of symmetry, he nonetheless had great environmental awareness, and his gardens—both public and private—bear the stamp of his unrivalled familiarity with the plant varieties adapted to their environment. For him, working with "living beings" was a "terrible responsibility."

The Garden of the Heart, Van Buuren Museum, Brussels, Belgium.

PIETRO PORCINAI

VVho is he?

Born in 1910, Pietro Porcinai vvas the son of the manager of one of Italy's finest gardens—
the Villa Gamberaia in Fiesole, and found himself immersed in the world of plants from his
earliest years. The renowned artist and designer, who died in 1986, was one of the outstanding landscape architects of his day. He began his studies at the Regia Scuola Agraria
Media higher college of agriculture before vvorking for Martino Bianchi in Pistoia. He went
on to work in Belgium and Germany, making the acquaintance of famous nursery gardeners like the German Karl Foerster. He also met well-known European landscape architects
like the Britons Russell Page and Geoffrey Jellicoe and the Belgian René Pechère.

His vvork

Pietro Porcinai vvorked in a number of countries, notably alongside Renzo Piano
for the Centre Pompidou in Paris. He also worked in Berlin, in Abu Simbel in Egypt,
and in Saudi Arabia. In Italy, he vvas involved in designing the Pinocchio Park at
Collodi. He also collaborated with the Brazilian architect Oscar Niemeyer on
building the headquarters of the Mondadori publishing house in Segrate. He
designed many private gardens in his ovvn country, such as the Giardino della
Gherardesca near Florence, the Villa L'Apparita near Siena, where his tvvo masterpieces are the gardens of the Villa Il Roseto and the Villa Palmeriana. A founding member of the International Federation of Landscape Architects, in 1950
he vvas behind the founding of its Italian section, the Associazione Italiana di
Architettura del Paesaggio.

His philosophy

As heir to the classical garden tradition, and nonetheless highly innovative in the use of materials and plant species, Pietro Porcinai advocated true interdisciplinarity among architects,
urban planners, artists, and landscape designers. He vvas very environmentally avvare, notably
with regard to the use of vvater, seeking solutions adapted to his country's climate by preferring hardy native species. The intelligence of the visual effect of his gardens, closely bound
in vvith the architectural demands—such as the Villa Il Roseto garage stairs, cunningly concealed in the curve of a hedge—is the hallmark of a mind in control of a project's every aspect,
whether functional or aesthetic. His sense of lines, forms, and simple textures made him
a rigorous yet sensitive professional, who hoped for a revival of interest in gardens and
landscapes in his country.

The Villa Il Martello gardens, Florence, Italy.

MARTHA SCHWARTZ

Who is she?

The American landscape architect Martha Schwartz, born in 1950, was, until 2000, married to Peter Walker, one of the greatest modernist architects in the United States. She studied at the Harvard Graduate School of Design, and made a brilliant debut in the landscape world in 1979 by creating a garden with bagels, which she laid out in front of her home, thereby playing havoc with the traditional view of the garden, and provoking lively critical and scandalized reactions from her colleagues. This was her way of taking issue with "society's sentimental attitude towards nature." Held to be the creator of the conceptualist movement, running counter to any display of nostalgia, she developed the idea of a garden similar to the spatial installations of the exponents of land art or minimal art. Her innovative and often iconoclastic work is situated at the intersection of architecture, art, and landscape.

Her work

Martha Schwartz is in great demand the world over. Her extraordinarily colorful work is extremely wide-ranging, whether it be her spectacular Dublin Docklands project in Ireland— a huge red resin carpet covered with crimson sticks lending structure to a vast square—or the Mesa Arts Center designed in Arizona in 2005, or the memorable green seats in the Jacob Javits Plaza in Manhattan (1992). She also designed Kitagata Garden City in Japan in 2000, and the Dickenson Garden in Santa Fe, New Mexico in 1993.

Her philosophy

As an avid user of bright colors, Martha Schwartz has an instantly recognizable style. Obsessed with finding quick, pragmatic solutions, and critical of the artificial nature of urban gardens, she cannot abide pretense in any shape or form. Her role is not to produce "facsimiles" of nature, and her style has nothing to do with plants. Faithful to her background in the visual arts, she designs very colorful gardens, breaking with the gray of the city, by deliberately using imitation materials with an immediate chromatic effect. Moving on from designing objects in a landscape to modeling the landscape so as to turn it into an integrated artwork and space struck her as a perfectly logical step. Martha Schwartz drew inspiration from minimalist artists like Robert Morris and Donald Judd, who defined space in terms of seriality, saying how, through their ability to master large spaces with few gestures and materials, landscape architects have a lot to learn from the minimalists.

Schwartz does not attempt to transform the landscape; she is fond of using repetitive motifs and mostly plays around with the rhythms of forms and colors. She entirely recreates a profoundly original decor, imposing a radically different view, recreating extraordinarily colorful scenes, as in the six open-air micro-gardens that she designed in El Paso, Texas. Her determination to make a clean break, and the provocative, humorous nature of many of her projects, have often caused controversy, which she accepts philosophically; for her, humor is far from frivolous and can be an effective way of making a serious point—as she points out, one only has to look at the audience that comedians attract as opposed to the much smaller following of doomsday preachers!

Splice Garden, an artificial garden designed by Martha Schwartz at the Whitehead Institute, Cambridge, United States: a contemporary combination of a Zen garden and an Italian Renaissance garden.

MIREI SHIGEMORI

Who is he?

From his teenage years, Mirei Shigemori (1896–1975) was interested in ike-bana (the Japanese art of flower arranging) and the tea ceremony. Hoping to become a painter, he studied Western art at the fine art university in Tokyo, and was influenced by European avant-gardes. Following the Tokyo earth-quake of 1923, he settled in Kyoto, where he studied the traditional arts. In 1931, he founded an ikebana institute, offering strict and varied training in subjects like art, aesthetics, and philosophy. From 1930 to 1932, he pub-lished many learned books on "the art of flower arrangement," and on tradi-tional Japanese gardens, of which he became an eminent specialist. In 1949, he founded a magazine devoted to flower arrangement.

His work

Apart from his many books, Shigemori designed 240 gardens of timeless beauty: *karesansui*, or dry landscape gardens, which offer a remarkable synthesis between tradition and a contemporary view. Among the highlights of his output is the Tofuku-ji in Kyoto (1939), which he restored with total creative freedom.

His philosophy

Mirei Shigemori brilliantly embodies the double postulate of the contempo-rary Japanese garden, at the crossroads of tradition and openness to Western influences. With his atypical career, he viewed gardens as visual artworks and his designs made him an artist like no other.

   His watchword was to be "eternally modern," and in this he was undoubt-edly successful. He was nicknamed "the Japanese Mondrian" on account of his patterns of crisscrossing lines, which he claimed to have used before the Dutch painter did. His designs rely principally on arrangements of erect stones and graphic patterns. He showed less interest in vegetation—by definition ephemeral. Shigemori also avoided the classic integration of the garden within the surrounding countryside, going as far as deliberately enclosing it behind walls.

Skillfully raked gravel in a contemporary karesansui designed by Mirei Shigemori, Kyoto, Japan.

JACQUES SIMON

Who is he?

An exceptional character, born in 1929 to a forester father—who passed on to him his passion for trees and the land—Jacques Simon is a two-time winner of the Grand Prix du Paysage (in 1990 and in 2006), and studied at the École des Beaux-Arts de Montréal and at the French national college of landscape architecture, the École Nationale Supérieure du Paysage, in Versailles. This indefinable artist has played a key role in the landscaping world in France.

His endless curiosity and inexhaustible energy turned this man with an unusual career into a great traveler, combining work as a publisher, author, and teacher, in France, Canada, and the United States. At once a poet and an artist, he has always stood apart through his humor, his extreme sensitivity, and his distancing in terms of established systems.

He started out with the Urbanisme et Architecture studio, working on new town projects and all kinds of urban development schemes, playgrounds, and small urban parks, where he was already firmly set in his determination to help the human side win out. Had it not always been his wish to "link man to the earth in his most basic action: the understanding of the great balances, the primary functions of life"?

Highly sensitive to traffic fluidity and simple forms, very early on he showed his concern for encouraging human encounters: "At the foot of the houses on the way to school, we need spaces for everyday use to excite, entertain, and inspire passing children to play, if only for a moment."

His work

Jacques Simon has designed many parks and gardens, in which his knowledge of plants enabled him to provide an answer to the "overwhelming desire" we all have for a "change of scenery without having to travel for miles." One of his great projects, exemplary in its handling of the environment, was the Parc de la Deûle in 2006, several thousand acres of farmland located at the boundary between the mining country and Lille, the capital of the Nord-Pas-de-Calais region of northern France.

His philosophy

Jacques Simon is one of those artist landscape architects who have never had any compunction in moving mountains, both figuratively and literally. For him, to create a park is "to respond to a population's need for contact with the natural elements, trees, water, earth and stone." Being highly sensitive to the material offered by vegetation, he considers that "the tree, the shrub, as living materials, offer a great many shapings of space … to model and structure the environment without disfiguring it." He holds that there is "an ongoing dialogue between the tree and the soil, between the tree and the sky." For him, the tree is not content just to be a set of timber and leaves: "It is a line of force in the landscape."

Simon is also a great "articulture" specialist. He is now fond of writing signs and words on the land, the way distant ancestors or very ancient civilizations inscribed mysterious shapes or unusual messages on the surface of our globe. A deeply generous utopian, connected to the sky, he guides the peasant or the tractor as if he could see the ground from above, with an acute and almost divinatory sense of the forms and dimensions about to appear; he sows his aphorisms in the corn or snow, turning the countryside into an extraordinary ephemeral "living" museum.

Exercise in "articulture" in the middle of a field of colza.

VLADIMIR SITTA

Who is he?

Born in Brno, in the former Czechoslovakia, Vladimir Sitta first studied landscape architecture in his native country, moving to West Germany—where he lived from 1979 to 1981—then emigrating to Australia. He settled in Sydney, where he has lived ever since.

His work

A multifaceted character, the designer of large gardens like the Garden of Australian Dreams at the National Museum of Australia in Canberra, or Fusionpolis in Singapore. He also works happily on more conventional gardens in Australia, with patios and swimming pools, without abandoning his natural boldness. His invariably very innovative designs are often seen as being iconoclastic. His landscape development plans have won numerous design awards and competitions.

His philosophy

Vladimir Sitta combines modern minimalism with baroque theatricality. For him, the garden is a huge stage, and its natural scenery is complemented with visual effects obtained notably with the four elements. He likes to play with fire, earth, air, and water. A perfectionist and theater lover, who would have liked to become an actor and who praises Fellini to the sky, knows how to get the best out of any surface area, be it a small secret garden in a city center, planted with bamboos haloed in mist, or grand landscapes recreated to recall the history of the Aborigines, as in the Garden of Australian Dreams in Canberra. But Sitta is also very fond of designing "imaginary" gardens and vying with nature in this way.

Sitta is considered a visionary with respect to urban gardens, in which he gives a free rein to his natural boldness.

With a truly cross-disciplinary approach to gardens, he manipulates forms, colors, lights, and textures, with lines of force that most often belong more to the realm of sculpture than to that of horticulture.

Sensitive to what is happening to the planet, his postulate is that "the earth is a non-renewable resource," and that cities ought to be self-maintaining and repair the damage inflicted on the countryside. To this end, he uses roof gardens and vertical gardens, which have the advantage of cooling the temperature and reducing pollution.

He claims to be a romantic: "Maybe all gardens seem romantic to us because we think that they will outlive us. I will not say that I am a dyed-in-the-wool romantic. Maybe what is romantic in me is that I believe that my gardens can have a positive effect."

Colored, asymmetrical steps in a private garden in Sydney, Australia.

PETER WALKER

Who is he?

An American architect born in California in 1932, Peter Walker studied at the University of California, Berkeley. Initially a journalist, he turned to landscape architecture in 1955, and studied at the University of Illinois with Stanley White. He studied at the Harvard Graduate School of Design, obtaining a master's degree in landscape architecture in 1957.

At Harvard, Walker was deeply influenced by his professor, Hideo Sasaki, a leading landscape architect, and was also able to work with Lawrence Halprin. After graduating, Walker worked for Sasaki, acquiring some invaluable work experience with the top landscape architects. Soon afterwards they formed a partnership as Sasaki, Walker, and Associates in 1957, until they parted company, with Peter Walker setting up Peter Walker and Partners in 1983, and developing a firm of international standing employing some thirty to forty landscape architects. In 2004, Peter Walker won the highest possible distinction: the Geoffrey Jellicoe Gold Medal from the International Federation of Landscape Architects.

His work

Peter Walker and Partners have developed numerous projects in the United States and throughout the world. The agency is responsible for the highly symbolic World Trade Center memorial in New York City with, in the middle, two large voids recalling the lost towers. He also designed works at the Toyota City Art Museum, the McConnel Foundation, the Nasher Sculpture Center Foundation, the Sony Center in Berlin, the IBM Solana Park in Dallas, Harvard's Tanner Fountain, Burnett Park, Jamison Place in Portland, Oregon, buildings and gardens for Bayer SA in Leverkusen, and for the Deutsche Post AG office in Bonn. He was also involved with the Mies-Van-der-Rohe-Strasse project in Munich, with Munich airport, with the Kempinski Hotel Airport in Munich, and more.

His philosophy

The projects of Peter Walker and his team are often productions on the scale of the broader landscape and are characterized by their minimalism, inspired by the French formal garden, an influence that the landscape architect openly lays claim to. Also influenced by abstraction and land art, Peter Walker sees art as a continual source of inspiration. Thus he has designed graphic and powerful works (attaching extreme importance to drawing and to plant and mineral textures), enabling him to "transfigure places' nature and form."

Gardens on the IBM Solana campus, Westlake and Southlake, Texas, United States.

WANG SHU

Who is he?

The architect and professor Wang Shu, born in Urumqi in the Xinjiang region in 1963, earned his first diploma in architecture in 1985, and his master's degree in 1988, from the Nanjing Nan Institute of Technology.

In 1997, Wang Shu and his wife Lu Wenyu founded their agency, Amateur Architecture Studio, in Hangzhou, China. After studying architecture in Nanjing, Wang Shu did a doctoral degree in urbanism. Now the dean of the China Academy of Art's Architecture Department, Wang Shu is regularly called upon to join panels of assessors abroad. He is notably a member of the appointments committee for the Ordos 100 project. Before becoming an architect, Wang Shu was a writer, and kept saying that he thought that architecture was only one part of his work. "Humanity is more important than architecture, and low-tech more important than hi-tech," he writes.

The work of his Amateur Architecture Studio agency has been shown at joint exhibitions in Berlin, Paris, and Rotterdam. Wang Shu and his wife have also received many awards: the Architecture Art Award of China in 2004; the Holcim Asia-Pacific Region Prize (the Holcim Foundation for Sustainable Construction) in 2006; the First International Prize for Sustainable Construction from the Cité de l'Architecture et du Patrimoine, Palais de Chaillot, Paris, in 2007, and in 2008 was short-listed for the prize for international best skyscraper in Frankfurt, Germany.

In 2010, a special mention from the panel of assessors was awarded to Déclin d'un Dôme (Decline of a Dome) by the Amateur Architecture Studio agency at the 12th Venice Biennale of Architecture. In 2012, his entire work was honored by the Pritzker Prize, a prestigious award considered the Nobel Prize for architecture.

His work

Among other architectural and landscape projects, Wang Shu's work in China includes Wenzheng College Library at Suzhou University (2000), the Ningbo Contemporary Art Museum (2005), Five Scattered Houses in Ningbo (2003–06), the campus of the Xiangshan China Academy of Art (from 2004 to 2007), the Ceramic House in Jinhua (2006), the Ningbo History Museum (2008), and the Exhibition Hall of the Imperial Street of Southern Song Dynasty in Hangzhou (2009).

To mark the tenth Venice Biennale of Architecture in 2006, Wang Shu installed, on a bamboo structure, sixty-six thousand tiles taken from demolished buildings in the Hangzhou region. The Tiles Garden is to be seen as a manifesto advocating recycling and the reinterpretation of traditional techniques. In 2012, Wang Shu designed a garden in Chaumont-sur-Loire as part of the International Garden Festival: the Jardin des Nuées Qui S'Attardent (Garden of Hanging Clouds).

His philosophy

Amateur Architecture Studio explores the relationship between the evolution of architecture, landscape, and ways of life in China. Wang Shu has a talent for reusing and poetically transposing traditional Chinese know-how into contemporary architectural language. Wang Shu has a special interest in Chinese vernacular architecture, which is inexpensive, spontaneous, and often transient. He takes a close interest in the problem of the massive destruction and reconstruction of Chinese cities. He bases his thinking on ancestral building methods under contemporary conditions while respecting traditional conceptions. He is very attached to the interdependence of architecture and landscape. His work also focuses on the reinterpretation of traditional architecture and respecting the environment.

The Ningbo Museum gardens, Ningbo, China.

JACQUES WIRTZ

Who is he?

Born in Antwerp in 1924, the Belgian landscape architect Jacques Wirtz studied landscape architecture and horticulture at the Tuinbouwschool in Vilvorde, northern Belgium. He began his career in 1948 and since 1950 has been a landscape architect in Schoten, Belgium. With his sons Peter and Martin now helping out, he is still working both with his agency and at the nursery he set up near his home, supervising all the projects linked to his name.

His work

Jacques Wirtz has designed over a hundred public and private gardens in Belgium, Britain and France. In particular, he was commissioned to do the Jardin du Carrousel project in the Tuileries Gardens in Paris, has worked on the presidential gardens of the Élysée Palace, and designed a walled water garden at Alnwick Castle in Northumberland, northern England. He designed the gardens for Antwerp's university hospital; he also did the design for the plots at the International Garden Festival in Chaumont-sur-Loire. He has worked extensively in Japan, Italy, Switzerland, Spain, Portugal, and the United States.

His philosophy

Jacques Wirtz has an in-depth knowledge of plants, having received a formal education in farming; he has developed an infinite passion for plant life, inciting him to constantly seek out new species, which he acclimatizes before using them in his gardens. Wirtz owes his fame to his topiaries, reinventing the technique with outstanding creativity. With his extremely virtuoso trimming of box, hornbeam, yew, and beech, he uses his incredible creative freedom to design eminently sculptural shapes. In modeling perspectives in hedges and beds, Wirtz demonstrates a superior art of composition and harmony, playing subtly on rhythms and repetitions.

Although his talent is not limited to his topiary skills, Jacques Wirtz has breathed new life into this area, as well as a flexibility and inventiveness never achieved before. With an unfailing eye, a remarkable sense of proportions, and an incredibly sure and expert hand, he invented the fluffy hedge, whose beauty in motion plays amazingly with the light and with the seasons.

Playing on the contrast between free forms of deciduous species and strictly formal box, often using hedges in stairs and herbaceous borders that winter will rust, he plans his high-brow play of color and calculated effect of spaces and forms in advance. Jacques Wirtz is the very epitome of the landscape architect intimately bound up in a long tradition, which he reinterprets with an extremely contemporary sensibility.

Rows of topiary in Jacques Wirtz's private garden, Belgium.

10

24 MUST-SEE GARDENS

Mas de Les Voltes,
a garden designed by
Fernando Caruncha,
Castel de Ampurdán,
Spain.

LITTLE SPARTA
Dunsyre (Scotland), United Kingdom

Little Sparta is an amazing garden, created in 1966 in Dunsyre near Edinburgh, on the desolate moorland of the Pentland Hills, by the artist, publisher, and poet Ian Hamilton Finlay.

This unusual garden is in itself an artistic, poetic, and philosophical work, a shrine of culture and horticulture. Little Sparta, which combines shady bosks with gardens opening onto the broader Scottish countryside, and dotted with stone, wooden, and metal bridges across streams and ponds decked with water lilies, is the theater for the historical and philosophical meditations of Ian Hamilton Finlay, an original and sometimes controversial artist, who died in 2006. Little Sparta bears the traces of Finlay's passion for antiquity, the French Revolution, and World War II, and offers the visitor a walk dotted with ruins, sculptures, and inscriptions carved in stone, which interact with the trees, the plants, and the wider landscape. Between the cascades and the drystone walls, there is a whole world of ferns, heather, hostas, willows, and wild geraniums that stretches before one's eyes. Faced with this highly evocative, deeply charming, and indefinable garden, the visitor cannot fail to be moved, by the garden's mystery, its poetry, and the dreamy wistfulness it provokes about the frailty of beings and of civilizations.

Engraved stones on the Scottish moors.

SÍTIO BURLE MARX
Barra de Guaratiba, Brazil

The Sitio Burle Marx is without doubt one of the world's most beautiful gardens. The work of the great Brazilian artist and landscape architect Roberto Burle Marx, this exceptional garden bears the hallmark of its author's genius. Passionate about plants, having taken part in numerous botanical expeditions in search of rare or poorly identified species, Roberto Burle Marx purchased the site in Santo Antonio da Bica Sitio, Barra de Guaratiba, in 1949, to house his plant collection and to continue acclimatizing the plants he had brought home from his travels. In 1973 he moved into the wonderful house located in the center of the site, next to a small sixteenth-century Benedictine chapel.

This extraordinary place, with a wealth of springs and valleys forming a beautiful setting, comprises over 3,500 plant species, and notably houses a remarkable collection of Bromeliaceae. Its luxuriant vegetation, play on colors, rare species, and walks under the palm fronds and among the orchids, cacti, and tree ferns—leading to poetic fountains and black stone steps—all make a visit to Sitio Burle Marx an unforgettable moment.

Sítio Burle Marx, the private garden of Roberto Burle Marx, near Rio de Janeiro, Brazil.

ROYAL BOTANIC GARDENS CRANBOURNE
Cranbourne (Victoria), Australia

The Red Sand Garden is a garden of outstanding beauty, designed as part of the botanical gardens in Cranbourne, near Melbourne. It was created by the landscape artists Taylor Cullity Lethlean and Paul Thompson, who exploit all the powers of stone, sand, and plants to take us into a universe beyond both time and space. This garden—intended to be viewed without entering—is graphically and chromatically effective like no other garden. The visitor is presented with an enormous tableau in warm colors, playing on every shade of red and beige, the colors of the Australian outback. The Cranbourne botanical gardens are designed in a very contemporary way, with a variety of settings using a broad range of plants suited to the desert conditions, Australia being situated in the world's driest continent. The list of materials used is also a very long one, both in the "red garden" and in the "arid garden," or in the other sections of this large, 897-acre (363-hectare) park: sand, pebbles, boulders, and flagstones of various colors play with the grays, blues, and gray-greens of the vegetation. Although following the logic of the dry landscape garden, the botanical richness at this park is truly impressive, and we see how, whether through its presence or through its absence, water shapes the landscape.

The spectacular Red Sand Garden at the Royal Botanic Gardens Cranbourne, near Melbourne, Australia.

JARDÍN ETNOBOTÁNICO DE OAXACA
Oaxaca, Mexico

The ethnobotanical garden in Oaxaca is an extraordinary garden, a combination of artistic sensitivity and scientific expertise. It was designed by an exceptional man, Francisco Toledo—a major Mexican contemporary artist who has turned his city into a museum and his garden into a work of art.

On a total surface area covering around 7 acres (3 hectares), close to 8,000 different species have been planted, altogether upwards of 900,000 plants belonging to 140 botanical families.

A committed artist, Francisco Toledo bears on his shoulders the defense of his city's heritage and the cause of art in every shape and form. "There were three books on painting in the entire city when I arrived here in 1952, and of course nothing on modern art. No galleries, no museums, and such poverty that quite naturally art was not a priority."

The garden he has created is of exceptional botanical diversity, evoking the Mexican people's relationship with plants. With Oaxaca possessing one of the richest ecosystems in the world, in this garden we find a large number of plant species, including, for instance, several kinds of cycads, agaves, and countless varieties of corn and peppers. But most importantly, it is a garden designed by an aesthete, who uses plants as a pictorial medium. He turns nature into the subject matter of his work, to create a uniquely fascinating visual world in which the cacti create magnificent plant scenes. Thus we can witness incredible Saguaro cacti, assembled like a host of spears pointing heavenward, toying effectively with the colors of the stones, the soil, and the water.

Raised spears of the Saguaro cactus in Francisco Toledo's Jardín Etnobotánico de Oaxaca, Mexico.

EXPERIMENTAL GARDEN
Méry-sur-Oise, France

This garden in Méry-sur-Oise is a remarkable experimental garden. In 1996, the French landscape architect Pascal Cribier, attracted by all the energies brought together at this one location—its history, the River Oise, the water coming from a new type of water-treatment facility using nanofiltration, and having a very low lime and chlorine content—proposed this experimental garden to the Vivendi Group. The story this garden tells, what it offers to the visitor's sensibility and reflection, is the tremendous diversity of relationships between plants and water, with the logic of these relationships dictating the garden's forms. Whether as rain, fog, or ice, through its mechanical, chemical, and thermal qualities, water is what shapes the vegetation. Thus three bosks, or groves—of morphology, mineralization (see images to the right), and latitudes—set out separately for the visitor things that in nature work alongside each other. On the edge of the flood plain, each one is seen against the light, in the dazzle of the water being diffracted in the light. Facing the château are two long rectangular ponds, the larger of which the engineers have contrived to set directly over the water table.

In the heart of the vast meadowland, a clump of white willows grows on the spot where a pond used to lie. The landscape architect insisted on keeping this witness to a lost orchard, which slightly changes the orientation of his new composition. While the presence of these willows is emblematic of the ability plants have to fit in with—and at the same time reveal—an environment, it is also symbolic of Cribier's approach, his project being anchored to the memory of the spot, whether it be human, geological, hydrological, or architectural.

This highly graphic and extremely creative garden, combining tarmac and vegetation, and including elements of botany, science, and sheer poetry, is really a garden that everyone must see, or rather ought to have seen, especially as it is now closed to visitors and under threat from lack of maintenance. In spite of this, it is undoubtedly one of the most extraordinary gardens of the last twenty years. Now in the hands of an organization that has stopped maintaining the wooded areas, it nonetheless continues to delight botany enthusiasts and to disassemble the peaceful autonomy of the plant world—with or without water.

The melancholy remains of an exceptional garden: before and after.

CÉSAR MANRIQUE'S GARDEN
Lanzarote, Spain

If you think that cacti are stiff and boring plants, hop onto a flight to the Canaries, where you will find an exceptional garden of euphorbia and succulents of every kind and in every shape and color. This garden was created by an irrepressibly fanciful artist in a sublime setting of volcanoes with their black earth, and mountains with their red soil.

César Manrique (1919–1992), a Spanish painter and a friend of the greatest artists of our times, after living for many years in New York City, decided in the late 1960s to go home for good to the island of his birth, where his environmental commitment led him to play a major role in conserving the island's beauty. This is how, in a setting that is now fully protected, he came to create the cactus garden in a wonderful natural amphitheater, which is listed by UNESCO as a World Biosphere Reserve and houses in its extraordinary setting of terraces, stones, and fountains, over ten thousand cactus plants in an incredibly diverse range of appearances and colors. The garden was also designed to be a cochineal farm, and amid the cultivation of the insects these natural sculptures of cactus—assembled as the inspired imagination of the garden's designer dictated—offer a display of surrealistic and stunning scenes.

Cacti tower majestically over a cinder area in César Manrique's garden, Lanzarote, Spain.

MAJORELLE GARDEN
Marrakech, Morocco

The Majorelle Garden was created in 1937 by the French painter Jacques Majorelle (1886–1962) in Marrakech, and was later the property of Yves Saint Laurent and Pierre Bergé. It is a must-see garden because of the very special harmony it derives from its unforgettable blue architecture and its collector's plants, imported from all over the world by the garden's founder. The bold, chromatic harmonies between the countless plants in the garden and the artist's villa walls take the visitor through an incredible symphony of colors and smells. If dreams have colors, they might very well be those of the Majorelle Garden: jade green pottery, bright yellow edging, and deep pink bougainvillea turn this garden into a paradisical interlude away from the bustle of the city. Exotic plants and rare species from all over the world have turned this garden into a luxuriant jungle populated with birds as well as cacti, yuccas, jasmines, palm trees, and bamboos. Ponds filled with water lilies, streams, and fountains plunge the visitor into an atmosphere of cool, calm, and forgetfulness.

It brings to mind these lines from the poet Charles Baudelaire: "There, there is nothing else but grace and measure/Richness, quietness, and pleasure."

Plant sculptures in the Majorelle Garden in Marrakech, Morocco.

ÉRIK BORJA'S ZEN GARDEN
Beaumont-Monteux, France

Érik Borja is an established authority on the design of Japanese-inspired gardens. His own garden in the Drôme département of southeastern France is the outcome of an original approach combining his Mediterranean roots and his personal take on the Zen garden concept.

A visual artist, he views the Japanese garden as a lexicon of forms, using the plants that he models—while expressing his aesthetic and spiritual impulses—in a fruitful dialogue with Nature, the main source of his inspiration. Érik Borja bases his work on the principles of feng shui, the ancient Chinese science practiced throughout the Far East.

Using all the traditional Japanese botanical vocabulary with art, science, and virtuosity—including maples and cherry trees, whose graceful forms emphasize the passing of the seasons both through the delicacy of their blossom in spring and through the flamboyance of their autumnal colors—he makes the garden a creator of emotions, a place of harmony and serenity par excellence. The pruning—poetic and precise—of the trees into flat shapes, clouds, *kokarikomi* (small bushes) or *okarikomi* (large bushes), while following the rules of Japanese topiary, reveals their hidden form and lends the garden its rigorous shape. Érik Borja is equally careful over the objects, stones, paving, paths, and cascades that give the perfect architecture of this garden its poetic rhythm.

This laboratory garden, which covers over 7 acres (3 hectares), with its Meditation Garden, Tea Garden, Stroll Garden, Cascade Garden, and Pond Garden combines mineral, vegetable, and aquatic atmospheres, and transports the visitor far beyond the boundaries of this peaceful estate in the Drôme region.

Cloud trees in Érik Borja's garden in the Drôme region, southeastern France.

INHOTIM BOTANICAL GARDEN
Brumadinho, Brazil

Inhotim, not far from Belo Horizonte, which was begun in the 1980s and opened to the public in 2006, is the largest botanical garden in Brazil and the largest open-air museum in Latin America. This extraordinary 3,000-acre (1,200-hectare) park is at once a huge garden (home, for example, to fifteen hundred different species of palm), and an outstanding contemporary art venue, with five hundred works by over a hundred artists from thirty different countries on display.

The wild dream of a wealthy collector with a passion for botany, this garden is both a tribute to the luxuriance of nature in Brazil and a gigantic outdoor museum, with nothing else quite like it. Works of some of the greatest artists of today can be found here—Anish Kapoor, Giuseppe Penone, Ernesto Neto, and Dominique Gonzalez-Foerster—in a world that seems to know no limits. One cannot help but marvel at the extraordinary diversity of plant life in this remarkably maintained and ordered spot, an outstanding setting for the art being created at present.

View of the extraordinary collection of palm trees at the Inhotim Botanical Garden, near Belo Horizonte, Brazil.

THE HIGH LINE
New York, United States

A public park designed on a disused rail line, the High Line straddles streets in western Manhattan. Owned by the City of New York, it is maintained by the Friends of the High Line, who fought for its preservation when it came under the threat of demolition. The first section of the High Line was officially opened in June 2009. In the space of a few years, this overhead line measuring more than 1 mile (2 kilometers) long has become a must-see venue in New York, completely out of character with the rest of the landscape and turning over a large part of the land to plant life.

In charge of plantings on the High Line, the Dutch landscape architect Piet Oudolf readily turned to plants that are suited to difficult and even hostile environments, and that will not suffer from seasonal changes, drought, or intense cold. He relies on self-seeding grasses and encourages especially hardy native species. As in all of Piet Oudolf's work, the chromatic harmonies of his plant scenes in the urban environment are particularly carefully executed, and offer within such a hectic city a breathing space that is unusually peaceful and extremely beautiful to boot.

When nature invades disused rail lines—the High Line in New York, United States.

LONGHOUSE RESERVE
East Hampton (New York), United States

LongHouse Reserve is a magnificent garden located in a forest in East Hampton, United States. Its creator, the world-renowned textile designer Jack Lenor Larsen, born in 1927, first conceived a passion for the shape and design of the plants he was collecting, and then decided to introduce into his garden art in all its various forms. Wondrous plants, as well as works inspired by the place—like Dennis Oppenheim's tar roses, Dale Chihuly's colored glass sculptures, and the works of designers like Andrée Putman—give rhythm to this inventive and eclectic world, which continues to grow bigger and better year after year.

The renowned red path at the LongHouse Reserve, East Hampton, United States.

JARDINS DE KERDALO
Trédarzec, France

The Jardins de Kerdalo in Trédarzec, Brittany, came about through the passion of the renowned botanist and painter Prince Peter Wolkonsky (1900–1997). Born in Russia and exiled to Paris in 1917, in the mid-1960s he was so taken with this spot in Brittany, not far from the town of Tréguier, and its acid soil that he created his extraordinary 42-acre (17-hectare) garden there. Taming the place with prodigious energy, logging, digging ponds and channels, with his artist's eye he gave structure to these hills, designing everything from terraces, footpaths, and cascades, to follies and grottoes. He composed flower beds with a truly scientific knowledge of color and an innate intuition for harmonies and associations of plants. He was especially sensitive to the beauty of the garden in winter, a season "when the outlines are revealed." Ponds covered with green duckweed, beds planted with perennials, grass and cobblestone squares forming checkerboard patterns, inspired by his trips, offer the visitor an original, poetic, secret universe laden with gunneras, azaleas, rhododendrons, clematis, Japanese maples, ferns, and rare hellebores. Many friends and personalities from the world of horticulture contributed to the beauty of this garden with their advice and their plants: Charles de Noailles, Jelena and Robert de Belder, Harold Hillier, Jean Cayeux, and Roger de Vilmorin. After Peter Wolkonsky's death in 1997, his daughter Isabelle and his son-in-law Timothy Vaughan, both landscape gardeners, brilliantly took over the accomplished work.

Delicate color harmonies in the shadow of giant gunnera in the Jardins de Kerdalo, Trédarzec, France.

JARDINS DE SÉRICOURT
Séricourt, France

The Jardins de Séricourt, designed by the landscape architect and nurseryman Yves Gosse de Gore, are deployed across a 10-acre (4-hectare) estate in northern France, and take the visitor along various paths, whether they be "Initiatory," "Nostalgic," or "Brick." They also lead the visitor into the Ephemeral Maze, Cathedral of Roses, and Shadow Wood—a whole secret, poetic universe drawn from the designer's imagination, and in which precious plants live in harmony alongside wild plants. Four hundred varieties of boxwood, yews, perennials, grasses, and hellebores live in this green paradise, which this plant artist has been passionately carving since 1985. Paying attention to detail as much as to the overall views, to shade as much as to light, to rhythms as much as to chance, Yves Gosse de Gore displays both rigor and fantasy, as well as his passion for lush foliage and topiaries in every shape and size—one need only think of his armies of disciplined yews. He has created an unforgettable setting, a reflection on his boundless green imagination.

The Cathedral of Roses in the Jardins de Séricourt, Séricourt, France.

GARDENS OF THE IMAGINATION
Terrasson, France

The Terrasson site, with its outstanding terraces, recalling the history of mankind through gardens, was designed by the American landscape architect Kathryn Gustafson in 1996. It is the archetype of the contemporary garden, resorting to every technical possibility currently available, though without losing the charm and emotion that one traditionally seeks in nature. The Sacred Forest, Plant Tunnel, Elementary Gardens, Green Theater, Axis of the Winds, Rose Garden, as well as perspectives, water gardens, and topiary: all of these are themes and places wavering between nature and architecture, which here symbolize nature in its most varied states. Add to these cascades and the magic of the endless play of water, colors, and smells—everything in Terrasson is designed to fill the visitor with wonderment.

Water fountains in the Gardens of the Imagination, Terrasson, France.

TOFUKU-JI TEMPLE GARDENS
Kyoto, Japan

The gardens of the well-known Tofuku-ji temple were laid out and recreated by the great Japanese landscape architect Mirei Shigemori (1896–1975). Made of gravel and rocks, matching the concrete, they feature geometric shapes and contrasts of colors, combined and composed with the utmost care. The expressive power of the gardens and their extraordinary blend of tradition and modernity come in for constant praise. Tofuku-ji is undoubtedly Mirei Shigemori's most spectacular design.

The Garden of Eight Phases, referring to the eight phases in the life of Buddha, features white gravel, representing the sea, and some powerful erect stones evoking the Islands of the Immortals, a classic theme in Zen gardens. Five mossy hillocks correspond to the major Rinzai temples. To the west, some horizontal rocks form a grid with the white gravel and azalea bushes. In the north garden, flagstones create a checkerboard pattern, recalling both the artist Piet Mondrian and traditional Japanese motifs. Lastly, the Great Bear Garden reuses stones from the temple to create the first-ever constellation pattern depicted in a Japanese garden.

Checkerboard pattern of moss and stone designed by Mirei Shigemori, Kyoto, Japan.

CHÂTEAU DE PANGE GARDENS
Pange, France

Like all of the works created by the landscape architect Louis Benech, the gardens of the Château de Pange, in the Moselle region of eastern France, bear the stamp of an especially elegant composition and some extremely gentle and poetic atmospheres. Clean lawns and flowered meadows, trimmed topiaries and wild grasses set off the surrounding landscape remarkably well, bringing nature up around the château, in a "green ocean" extending as far as the eye can see. Garden rooms and meadows of supple grasses subtly alternate and turn this place into an extraordinary garden in the country just as much as "the country in a garden." The play on colors, especially the greens, and on vistas—notably thanks to the flowered island turned into a feature by the landscape architect, which modify relations of scale and place the garden magnificently in its environment—give this garden a charm all of its own. Its sober lines, its extreme sensitivity, its inventiveness with plants, and a remarkable sense of harmony make the Pange gardens an unforgettable place.

Subtle plant harmonies in the garden paths of Château de Pange, Pange, France.

GIARDINI LA MORTELLA
Forio (Ischia), Italy

The botanical gardens of La Mortella, developed by the well-known British composer Sir William Walton and his Argentinian wife Susana, are on the island of Ischia, Italy, occupying a huge volcanic rock that dips down toward the sea. They are the handiwork of the great British landscape architect Russell Page. The garden enjoys the benefit of the extraordinarily fertile soil found on the island, which has luxuriant vegetation, with a profusion of woods, pine forests, vineyards, and lemon trees—hence Ischia's nickname, "the green island."

This name's significance really becomes apparent at Forio, where the La Mortella gardens are located. The park contains over eight hundred rare and exotic plant species scattered around a veritable maze of footpaths on the hillside.

An upper garden, called the "Hill," and a lower garden, called the "Valley," take the visitor round a fascinating labyrinth of dips, paths, and undergrowth populated with pine trees, tree ferns, and collector's ginkgo bilobas. The nearby Nymphaeum—a formal garden with a memorial to Susana Walton—shelters some generous groups of myrtle, rock roses, and lavender, adding their delightful scents to the air, cooled by numerous fountains and cascades. Designed with taste, rigor, and inventiveness, this garden is definitely one of Russell Page's most poetic projects.

The ponds and fountains of Giardini La Mortella, Foria, on the island of Ischia, Italy.

BOIS DES MOUTIERS
Varengeville-sur-Mer, France

Created around a hundred years ago in the Arts and Crafts style by the architect Edwin Lutyens and the English landscape designer Gertrude Jekyll at the request of the then owner Guillaume Mallet, the house and gardens at the Bois des Moutiers are in every way outstanding. Home to some extraordinary plant collections, the gardens, in a small dry valley that runs down to the sea between two cliffs, have a rich, acidic soil in which Himalayan rhododendrons, Chinese azaleas, Japanese maples, and all kinds of hydrangeas thrive. The place has a special atmosphere—magical, mysterious, and serene—which gives the gardens an extraordinary charm, whatever the season. It has garden rooms (*chambres de verdure*) and the famous mixed borders, beds bound by boxwood and containing some extraordinary floral compositions in masterfully controlled colors, illustrating Gertrude Jekyll's idea that any garden can and should become a "work of art." In the understory beneath the Atlas cedars, beech, and pines, we also find a string of clearings adorned with spectacular rhododendron bushes, impressively huge and bewitchingly colorful—fascinating clouds of pink and red. A wonderful place to meditate, the Bois des Moutiers is undoubtedly one of the world's most beautiful gardens.

White rhododendrons in the mists of the Bois des Moutiers, Varengeville-sur-Mer, France.

HIDCOTE MANOR
Hidcote Bartrim (England), United Kingdom

Hidcote Manor in the Cotswolds (Gloucestershire) was designed by a great traveler who was keen on plants—the British officer Major Lawrence Johnston (1871–1958)—in the early twentieth century. He was doubtless influenced by Alfred Parsons and Gertrude Jekyll. This garden has twenty-eight garden rooms surrounded by walls, yew, box, and holly hedges, to protect the plants from the wind and cold. The garden's highly structured architecture, the carefully trimmed topiaries, the great abundance of the inner beds brimming with unusual and exotic plants brought in from all parts of the globe, favored a microclimate that enabled all sorts of gardening experiments to be carried out. Breaking the established rules, and in particular flouting traditional color schemes, since he dared to use reds and large perennials at the front of his flower beds, Johnston invented a free form of garden which became a source of inspiration for many landscape gardeners. Bequeathing his garden to the National Trust in his own lifetime, Johnston went on to produce another magnificent garden: the Serre de la Madone, in Menton on the French Riviera.

Garden rooms in the snow at Hidcote Manor, Hidcote Bartrim, United Kingdom.

JARDIN DE LA LOUVE
Bonnieux, France

The Jardin de la Louve is a minimalist work created in Bonnieux, in the south of France, by Nicole de Vésian (1916–1996), a stylist with Hermès specializing in textiles. One day she decided to put her gifts to a different use, by working with live material—namely plants—and creating a three-dimensional tapestry. This precious garden, composed of terraces up the hillside, in perfect osmosis with the surrounding countryside, is a delicate mixture of stones and carved trees, with only a few botanical varieties, and it subtly plays with shapes and colors—grays, greens—and the Mediterranean light. An invitation to quiet and peacefulness, this poetic artist's garden, with its abundance of various boxwoods, arbutus, olive trees, santolina and rosemary, is currently owned by Judith Pillsbury, a Paris-based print dealer and a great garden lover. The archetypal modern Mediterranean garden, La Louve, with its admirable velvety green bushes, is a benchmark garden for many a contemporary landscape architect.

Clipped box in the Jardin de la Louve, Bonnieux, France.

SISSINGHURST CASTLE GARDEN
Sissinghurst (England), United Kingdom

Sissinghurst Castle garden was created in the 1930s next to a large Elizabethan manor house by the writer Vita Sackville-West (1892–1962) and the diplomat and journalist Harold Nicolson (1886–1968). These two larger-than-life personalities put a great deal of their energy into developing this exceptional spot, comprising ten different gardens. Thus, a number of different "garden rooms" were laid out from year to year, including a Herb Garden, a Spring Garden of mostly yellows, a Cottage Garden, and a legendary White Garden, with its numerous shades of white, gray, and green. White peonies, foxgloves, gypsophilas, hydrangeas, Chinese bellflowers, climbing roses, white buddleias, and old almond trees—all the light-colored plants are brought together here to create a uniformly white universe. Another legendary creation is the creeping Thyme Lawn, whose softness and sweet smells contribute to the place's reputation. One unusual aspect of the Sissinghurst garden is that its creators designed it as if they lived there; the garden rooms, created by the walls and hedges, were in fact arranged and interconnected like rooms in a large house, hence the extreme elegance and refinement of the whole estate. The diaphanous bushes and hornbeam hedges at Sissinghurst make it an unforgettable garden.

Arbor of white roses in the garden at Sissinghurst Castle, near Cranbrook, United Kingdom.

AWAJI YUMEBUTAI BOTANICAL GARDEN
Awaji (Hyogo), Japan

Awaji Yumebutai is a huge tiered garden designed by the Japanese architect Tadao Ando as part of a reclamation scheme involving a hill damaged by human activity. The park, which was not included in the initial plan, was added following the Kobe earthquake. The vast expanse of flowered terraces, which vary from season to season, and the 250,000 trees planted when very small (4 inches/10 centimeters high) have gradually taken up a dominant place in the overall scheme, in which water, earth, and constructed spaces are a celebration of nature. The work began in 1997 and was completed in March of 2000, covering over 23 acres (9.5 hectares). As Tadao Ando himself states, "the scenario is constantly changing and, especially for landscape, such a project cannot be described as a definitive operation." This giant multicolored grid of square flower boxes linked by stairs is an excellent example of graphically powerful landscaping.

Geometric terraces designed by Tadao Ando, Awaji, Japan.

GARDEN OF COSMIC SPECULATION
Holywood (Dumfriesshire, Scotland), United Kingdom

Designed by Charles Jencks (born in 1939), an American architect based in Scotland, and his wife Maggie, the amazing Garden of Cosmic Speculation is their private garden, located at their residence Portrack House. Jencks is a theoretician of postmodernism; his garden covers 40 acres (16 hectares) and offers a spectacular meditation on the cosmos and the laws of nature. Spiral hills covered with the green velvet of impeccable lawns, water mirrors reflecting the heavens, distorted black-and-white checkerboards, unlikely mazes, the twisted arches of red bridges dotted around the park's footpaths, a strange double spiral stairway into the water—everything in this quirky and surprise-filled garden is conducive to meditation and daydreaming. This utopian reflection on contemporary discoveries in areas such as biology or chaos theory, transcribed in spatial terms, leaves the visitor fascinated with the green transposition of scientific theories. But however zany and esoteric it may be, a garden is definitely what it is, with its Snake Mound and Snail Mound—the visitor will take home an indelible memory of climbing skywards up their gentle slopes. Charles Jencks's garden is unquestionably one of the most original gardens of our time.

The gentle hills of Charles Jencks's garden at Portrack House in Scotland.

PARC DE LA VILLETTE
Paris, France

The Parc de la Villette, designed by the Swiss-born French architect Bernard Tschumi, who won the architectural competition in 1983, is a vast urban park covering 136 acres (55 hectares) on the site of the former covered market at La Villette. Composed of large meadows and theme gardens, the Parc de la Villette was devised "as a theoretical and conceptual reflection on nature's place in a city in the postindustrial age." Its originality lies partly in the fact that it is not enclosed, but remains open day and night. It is also a major venue for cultural activities and an attraction for all sections of the general public. Bernard Tschumi based the park layout design on a triple system of lines, points, and surfaces. The line system is traced by two main north–south and east–west axes. The points system is marked out by the twenty-six contemporary follies, all different, their sumptuous red color dotted around the park. The surfaces system comes in the shape of two very large meadows: the Prairie du Triangle and the Prairie du Cercle.

The Parc de la Villette includes numerous theme gardens, taking the form of a cinematic walk, with garden lounges, play areas, and rest areas. The gardens are called the Jardin des Bambous (Bamboo Garden), the Jardin des Voltiges (Acrobatics Garden), the Jardin des Dunes (Sand Dune Garden), the Jardin des Miroirs (Mirror Garden), the Jardin des Ombres (Shadow Garden), the Jardin des Équilibres (Garden of Equilibria), the Jardin des Treilles (Arbor Garden), the Jardin des Frayeurs Enfantines (Garden of Childhood Fears), the Jardin des Dragons (Dragon Garden), and the Jardin des Îles (Garden of Islands)—gardens to experience and daydream about.

Wide, open spaces in the heart of the city at the Parc de la Villette, Paris, France.

APPENDIXES

KEY DATES

1862
CHELSEA FLOWER SHOW
Every year in London since 1862, for five days in the third week in May, the world's number one gardening event has been held in the gardens of the Royal Hospital in Chelsea. Organized by the Royal Horticultural Society, it enables horticulturists to present their best work of the year. Ten contemporary gardens are on display on this occasion.

1948
FOUNDING OF THE IFLA
Founding of the International Federation of Landscape Architects (IFLA) by the English landscape architect Geoffroy Jellicoe (1900–94).

1981
FLORENCE CHARTER
Drafted in 1981 by the International Committee for Historic Gardens, this charter related to the preservation of historic gardens, as an addendum to the Venice Charter (setting out universal guidelines regarding the preservation and restoration of monuments and art objects). It includes recommendations on the maintenance, conservation and restoration of gardens of interest to the public from an artistic or historical point of view.

1982
LES JOURNÈES DES PLANTES À COURSON (COURSON PLANT FESTIVAL)
This plant festival near Paris, first held in 1982 on the initiative of Hélène and Patrice Fustier, is a must for all lovers of high-quality rare plants.

1983
BUNDESGARTENSCHAU (BUGA)
A major event held at different venues in Germany, bringing together landscape architects and horticulturists, and which has taken place in Munich, Stuttgart, and Rostock.

1992
CHAUMONT-SUR-LOIRE INTERNATIONAL GARDEN FESTIVAL
Founded in 1992, this annual festival presents a panorama of creative landscape gardens and architecture throughout the world.

1999–2000
LE JARDIN PLANÉTAIRE EXHIBITION
Held at La Villette, in Paris, this widely acclaimed exhibition was curated by Gilles Clément. It sought to show how the Planetary Garden is a representation of the Earth, which should be treated like a garden in order to preserve its biodiversity.

Dew Garden by Chris Parsons, Aylesbury, United Kingdom.

Carpet of *Montia siberica* among a grove of katsura trees, designed by Russell Page
for the arboretum in Kalmthout, Belgium.

GLOSSARY

ALLOTMENTS
Gardens grouped together on the outskirts of towns and rented out by private companies or municipalities.

ARBOR
A garden construction comprising a shady shelter covered with climbing plants.

ARTS AND CRAFTS
A late nineteenth-century British art movement aimed at rehabilitating manual labor and traditional techniques, to which the landscape designer Gertrude Jekyll (1843–1932) was especially close. Her collaboration with the architect Edwin Lutyens (1869–1944) is illustrated by the Bois des Moutiers in Varengeville-sur-Mer, France. The Hidcote Manor garden in the United Kingdom was also inspired by this movement.

BIODIVERSITY
The diversity of living animal and plant species, whose preservation is a vital component of sustainable development. The growing awareness of the extinction of a considerable number of species has turned the protection and restoration of living things into one of the cornerstones of ecology.

BIOTOPE
A natural space in which given animal and plant species can develop freely.

CHARMILLE
A hornbeam hedge, bower, arbor, or tree-lined walk.

COMPOSTING
The recovery of plant waste (leaves, grass mowings, and clippings), which is turned into a soil improver by fermentation, and used to enhance soil fertility.

DERELICT URBAN LAND
Corresponds to what used to be known as waste ground. These are uncultivated plots, either because they have never been cultivated, or because earlier cultivation has been discontinued.

DRY LANDSCAPE GARDEN
An environmentally friendly garden requiring no watering and no fertilizer.

ESPALIER
A fence against which fruit trees are trained.

FALLOW LAND
Land left abandoned, following the ending of some farming, port, or industrial activity.

FAMILY GARDENS
Plots, often managed by an association, which are tended by amateur gardeners to meet the needs of their family.

FENG SHUI
A key feature of the traditional Chinese garden. This principle seeks to balance the forces of nature, of the harmony between man and his environment, meaning literally means "less is better," thereby placing quality before quantity. It leads to discovering the main elements of the garden environment and locating its negative and positive aspects, as the garden is where this osmosis occurs as man and nature meet.

FOLLY
An ornamental structure (e.g., summerhouse, pavilion, ruin), introduced into gardens during the eighteenth century and intended as decorative and whimsical features.

GREEN ARCHITECTURE
Environmentally friendly architecture, as seen from a sustainable development perspective.

GREEN SPACE
A park space, from the very small to the very large, that contains vegetation in an urban environment.

GREENWAY
A green area linking neighborhoods or villages, which gives preferential treatment to walkers and cyclists.

HERBACEOUS BORDER
Recurrent compositions in modern English gardens, herbaceous borders—also known as mixed borders—are areas made up of perennial plants and bulbs and annuals all mixed together, generally up against a wall or hedge. The chromatic effects are essential. Two of the most famous British mixed borders are at Great Dixter in East Sussex (southern England) and Hidcote Manor (Gloucestershire, southwest England).

KARESANSUI
A Japanese word meaning "dried-up landscape," that is used to describe dry landscape gardens of Zen Buddhist inspiration, composed of boulders set on carefully raked white gravel, and composing scenes conducive to meditation.

KITCHEN GARDEN

A garden originally intended for growing plants for the table, but which has also become a decorative place designed to be aesthetically pleasing.

MIXED BORDER

See Herbaceous Border.

MONOCHROME

A monochrome garden is a garden that plays with a whole range of shades of the same color. The White Garden at Sissinghurst in England is one of the best examples of this type of garden.

This Is Not Monochrome, Chaumont-sur-Loire International Garden Festival, 2009.

MOSAICULTURE

A garden decoration technique inspired by the art of the mosaic, and involving the mixing of plants of different colors and assembling them in geometric patterns.

MULCHING

A method for protecting plants by placing mulch (straw, peat, or bark) on the ground, both to prevent plants from dehydrating and to control weeds.

NATIVE PLANT SPECIES

Plants that grow naturally in the wild state in a given area.

PERENNIAL

Unlike annuals—plants that only live for one season—a perennial plant has a base that flowers several years in succession, even though the stems die back each year.

PERGOLA

A stone or wooden structure forming a shady path decorated with climbing plants, such as roses, jasmine, wisteria, or honeysuckle.

PHYTOREMEDIATION

A method that uses plants and microorganisms to remove pollutants from contaminated soils or waste water.

PLANETARY GARDEN

A concept invented by the French landscape architect Gilles Clément, drawing attention to the fragility of the plant world, its interdependence with the animal world, the planet being considered a single, huge garden that needs to be preserved.

PLANT PALETTE

A set of plant species and varieties adapted to the location and used in a garden or park, similar to the colors available to a painter on his palette.

PLEACHING

A method for maintaining hedges in the form of living fences by interlacing their branches, in particular to strengthen ageing hedges.

SENSITIVE NATURAL AREA

An area whose natural character is under threat and made vulnerable, either through urban pressure or the growth of economic or leisure activities, or on account of some particular interest, with respect to the quality of the site or the characteristics of the animal or plant species to be found there.

SHARED GARDENS

Gardens on a local level managed collectively by a group of people, with areas for them to come together and enjoy each other's company.

STROLL GARDEN

A Japanese garden style intended to be visited by following a path uncovering a succession of views. As a general rule, it involves a walk round a lake dotted with islands, bridges, and arbors.

SUSTAINABLE DEVELOPMENT

Development that meets the needs of present generations, without jeopardizing the ability of future generations to meet theirs.

TOPIARY

The art of training and trimming evergreen trees and shrubs, such as box or yew, into abstract or figurative shapes.

SELECTED BIBLIOGRAPHY

Baridon, Michel. *Les Jardins. Paysagistes, jardiniers poètes.*
Paris: Robert Laffont, 1999.

——. *Naissance et renaissance du paysage.*
Arles: Actes Sud, 2006.

Barlow Rogers, Elizabeth. *Landscape Design:
A Cultural and Architectural History.*
New York: Harry N. Abrams, 2001.

Brunon, Hervé, and Monique Mosser.
Le jardin contemporain. Paris: Scala, 2006.

Cauquelin, Anne. *L'Invention du paysage.*
Paris: Plon, 1989.

The Contemporary Garden.
London/New York: Phaidon Press, 2009.

Corajoud, Michel. *Le paysage, c'est l'endroit
où le ciel et la terre se touchent.*
Arles/Versailles: Actes Sud/ENSP, 2010.

Cribier, Pascal. *Itinéraires d'un jardinier.*
Paris: Éditions Xavier Barral, 2009.

Donadieu, Pierre. *Les Paysagistes.*
Arles: Actes Sud, 2009.

Frieze, Charlotte M. *Private Paradise:
Contemporary American Gardens.*
New York: The Monacelli Press, 2011.

Garraud, Colette. *L'Idée de nature dans l'art contemporain.*
Paris: Flammarion, 1994.

Gilles, Tiberghien. *Land Art.*
New York: Princeton Architectural Press, 1996.

Hill, Penelope. *Contemporary History of Garden Design:
European Gardens between Art and Architecture.*
Basel: Birkhäuser Architecture, 2000.

Hobhouse, Penelope. *In Search of Paradise:
Great Gardens of the World.*
London: Frances Lincoln, 2006.

Jellicoe, Geoffrey. *The Landscape of Man.*
London: Thames and Hudson, 1995.

Jones, Louisa, and Clive Nichols. *Mediterranean
Landscape Design: Vernacular Contemporary.*
London: Thames and Hudson, 2012.

Lassus, Bernard. *Hypothèses pour une troisième nature.*
Paris/London: Coracle Press, 1992.

Le Dantec, Jean-Pierre. *Jardins et paysages.*
Paris: Larousse, 1997.

——. *Poétique des jardins.*
Arles: Actes Sud, 2011.

Mosser, Monique, and Georges Teyssot.
*The History of Garden Design: The Western Tradition
from the Renaissance to the Present Day.*
London: Thames and Hudson, 2000.

Nicolin, Pierluigi, and Francesco Repishti.
Dictionary of Today's Landscape Designers.
Milan: Skira, 2003.

Oudolf, Piet, and Noël Kingsbury.
Landscapes in Landscapes.
New York: The Monacelli Press, 2011.

Pigeat, Jean-Paul. *Gardens of the World:
Two Thousand Years of Garden Design.*
Paris: Flammarion, 2003.

Racine, Michel, ed. *Garden and Landscape
Architects of France* (bilingual edition).
Oostkamp: Stichting Kunstboek, 2007.

Roger, Alain. *Court traité du paysage.*
Paris: Gallimard, 1994.

Spencer-Jones, Rae, and Elizabeth Scholtz.
1001 Gardens You Must See Before You Die.
New York: Barron's Educational Series, 2007.

Thébaud, Philippe. *Dictionnaire des jardins et paysages.*
Paris: Éditions Jean-Michel Place, 2007.

Tiberghien, Gilles. *Nature, art, paysage.*
Arles/Versailles: Actes Sud/ENSP, 2001.

Walker, Peter, and Melanie Simo. *Invisible Gardens:
The Search for Modernism in the American Landscape.*
Massachusetts: The MIT Press, 1996.

Weilacher, Udo. *In Gardens: Profiles of Contemporary
European Garden Architecture.*
Basel: Birkhäuser, 2005.

INDEX OF PROPER NAMES

Page numbers in bold refer to illustrations

Grand Canal Square by Martha Schwartz, Dublin, Ireland.

Private English garden.

Parc André-Citroën, designed by Allain Provost, Gilles Clément, Patrick Berger, Jean-Paul Viguier, and Jean-François Jodry, Paris, France.

PHOTOGRAPHIC CREDITS

The names of the designers of the gardens at Chaumont-sur-Loire can be found on the Web site of the Domaine de Chaumont-sur-Loire.

The author would like to thank the following people:

Élisabeth Couturier for her sound advice and constant wholehearted encouragement; Julie Rouart for her energy and unfailing enthusiasm; François Huertas for his remarkable visual inventiveness; François Barré, Louis Benech, Caroline de Sade, and Che Bing Chiu for their assistance and invaluable advice; Marion Doublet for her consideration and her persistent image research; Anne Dumond for her thought-provoking documentary research; Jean-Michel Dumond for his conscientious proofreading; Claire and Marie Dumond for their patience; as well as all those who have contributed to the completion of this work in one way or another.

RIGHT

*Coral Garden,
Chaumont-
sur-Loire
International
Garden Festival,
2008.*

FAR RIGHT

*Detail of
a garden
by Andy Cao.*

Translated from the French by John Lee
Design: François Huertas
Copyediting: Penelope Isaac
Typesetting: Thierry Renard
Proofreading: Chrisoula Petridis
Color Separation: Reproscan
Printed in Portugal by Printer Portuguesa

Originally published in French as *Jardin contemporain: mode d'emploi*
© Flammarion, S.A., Paris, 2012

English-language edition
© Flammarion, S.A., Paris, 2013

13 14 15   3 2 1

ISBN: 978-2-08-020143-0
Dépôt légal: 03/2013